INDESTRUCTIBLE

A LOVE STORY

SYLVESTER REYES

Blue Heron Book Works, LLC

Allentown, Pennsylvania

Copyright © 2025 Luis Moreno
All rights reserved.
Any similarity to persons living or dead is a coincidence.
No part of this book may be reproduced in any form without permission from the author or editor.
www.blueheronbookworks.com
ISBN: 979-8-99-13625-6-6

DEDICATION

Dedicated to my mother for taking the worst of it all, my rage, my pain, my suffering, when she had more than enough things in her life to worry about, no matter how horrible things got, she never gave up on me. I hope she can truly forgive me

Dedicated to my father, made me the man, the fighter, the DJ and father that I am today, your struggles in life to provide a decent life for us never went unnoticed and I'm so sorry for the lost time we had because of this fight I had to go through. I know it's time we'll never get back but we can continue to make up for it going forward and leaving this behind us

To Michael Robinson, the man behind the music. He stood side by side in silence with me during this decade long battle. All the late nights looking up legal loopholes we can apply to my cases, provided the majority of the finances for me to keep meeting with lawyers, counselors, etc. I'm sorry I lost the fight but I'm forever in your debt and I cannot put into words how thankful I am for all that you've done for me.

Contents

- DEDICATION iii
- ACKNOWLEDGMENTS v
- PROLOGUE 1
- INDIANAPOLIS 6
- WHY LILITH? 15
- LILITH SAYS, "I WANT MY MOMMY" 21
- THE WAR OF THE ROSES 27
- 2011 TRYING TO MAKE IT WORK 28
- TRUE LOVE ENTERS THE PICTURE: BIANCA 35
- GOING ON A CRUISE AND GETTING MARRIED 49
- HOW TO RUIN A GOOD THING 58
- THINGS UNRAVEL 65
- FINALLY, A WIN! 69
- ONCE MORE INTO THE TRENCHES 72
- THE BREAKUP WITH BIANCA 77
- 2016 ENDS WITH A BANG 79
- 2017 THINGS ARE LOOKING UP 84
- AND LOOKING DOWN AGAIN….2017 ENDS 92
- 2020 THE BEGINNING OF THE END 94
- WHAT HAPPENED NEXT 98
- WHAT'S NEXT—FROM THE EDITOR 103
- ABOUT THE AUTHOR 107

ACKNOWLEDGMENTS

Dear Paul,

I can't express to you how much our book sessions meant to me. After 26 counselors, you would be considered 27 and definitely my favorite one! I know these meetings between us were to discuss certain points about this book and how we wanted to approach it. We would branch off and discuss situations of our past and gaining any knowledge from you will forever be etched in my mind. The tears I shed telling you what I went through with losing my daughters made me feel more relief than any grad school so-called counselors I've ever met with.

The distractions in our conversations of how my Chicago Bulls of the 90s dominated your New York Knickerbockers always had us laughing and excited from a rivalry over 30 years ago! My favorite "off the topic" conversation!!

Thank you, Paul, from the bottom of my heart for being patient with me as I did my best to get through this journey. No matter where I got with my story, you and your wife will always be right there with me. When I eat at any of the diners we met at, our memories will forever play in my mind. You are and will always be truly missed. Rest in Paradise, Boss.

Sly

PROLOGUE
2021

It was a long day. I arrived at the courthouse at 9 o'clock with my Mom who flew in from Kentucky late the night before. The rest of my posse was there as well: Linda Sirop Vega, who had recently won a magisterial judgeship in Allentown; Jessica Lee Ortiz whose Ark Foundation helped dozens if not hundreds of families in Allentown get food and necessities during the pandemic lockdown; Sheila, the mother of our newborn twins; Bathsheba Monk, my editor and publisher. They all believed in me. Believed that I am a good father and deserved to have primary custody of my daughters, Lady and Sprout. They believed that my daughters would have a better shot at life if they lived primarily with me.

This court date was not, as they say, my first rodeo. I had taken my daughters' mother, Lilith, to court 36 times to the tune of $60,000 over the past 11 years. It started when Lillith was pregnant with Lady, my oldest. I had rented a small apartment for us and our new baby. But as soon as Lillith moved in, she declared our one-bedroom was too small and moved back into her mother's two-bedroom apartment, which was already housing 5 people. Then, when Lady was being born, Lillith wouldn't allow me in the delivery room. The delivery nurse had pity on me being denied one of life's biggest joys of seeing your child being born and snuck Lady out for me to hold briefly. I will always be grateful to her for that. Even so, after that, I had to go to court to be allowed to see my daughter and then to keep her mother from taking her out of state or to Puerto Rico as she threatened.

From the birth of Lady it was downhill. Lillith ran away with a family friend, Luke, who eventually ended up in jail for burglary, DUI, and receiving stolen goods. Nevertheless, she tried to keep Lady from me. I kept going to court to get someone to see Lillith wasn't a fit mother and even though I worked long hours—which, believe it or not, is considered a fault in the family court world, not the sterling trait it was when I was growing up—I was not considered suitable father material. Still, I kept up a good relationship with Lady. But this was going to be the last time I would put myself and my daughters through this. Fighting over them would have to be worse, in my opinion, than them living with their mother, even if their mother was making it increasingly hard to see my kids. In the past year, Lillith wouldn't produce Lady for our scheduled visits. I would come to the house and she would either be gone or didn't come out. Lillith said Lady refused to come with me. I could only imagine what her mother was telling her about me, because before this, we had always had a great relationship. In fact, when Luke was in jail for burglary, Lillith and I managed to communicate in a civilized manner and Lady and I had a great relationship. You can draw your own conclusions about that.

But the worst part was, I felt like I was being left out of my kids' life. Lillith wouldn't inform me when Lady was absent from school which was almost 22 days in one semester every year, and she wasn't keeping me informed about her mental state, which was increasingly deteriorating. She was depressed. Everything I read on the net told me that it was important for fathers to be a presence in a girl's life to help her when confronted with difficulties as well as how to cope with the aftermath of those difficulties. But how could I help if I had no contact with her?

This court date, though, I decided, would be my last. I was tired. I was broke…both from the lawyers and court fees—which I had taken out loans to cover—as well as mandatory child support, which I paid gladly but which was still keeping me from saving any money. And I figured: how could the justice system refuse to see that Lillith was continually in contempt of court, for which I provided mountains of receipts, and should therefore forfeit her rights to primary physical custody. Despite continual warnings from the judge, she refused to download the app that was to be our primary mode of communication because it was transparent to not only us, but the judge and the lawyers as well. She also refused to produce Lady for our visits. I am sure that not having contact with me was alienating my daughter's affections from me.

So, this was the last. I was confident. It was right before Christmas and the judge was about to retire, and he promised to have his order written before the holiday began. I began to have hope.

Because of Covid and distancing guidelines, the courtroom was closed. The judge allowed only one character witness in at a time, which was frustrating because I wanted everyone to hear what Lillith was saying. Hear what kind of lies she routinely told. And I wanted to hear what my kids were saying, but I was asked to leave while the judge interviewed them. Still, I was confident that finally, finally, *finally* the truth would come out, Lillith would be held in contempt, and I would win primary physical custody of Lady and Sprout, which I knew in my heart was the best thing for them. Someone asked me once, why I wanted kids so badly and the answer seemed so simple, I surprised myself. I imagined a bunch of kids running to see me when I came home from work and me spending time with them, playing with them and helping with their schoolwork. Maybe it was a substitute for the happy home life I missed out on, but for whatever reason, it was what I wanted more than anything. I never would have thought something so basic would be an almost impossible dream.

The hearing went on till the courthouse closed at five. My posse stayed with me the whole day, sneaking peaks into the narrow windows of the courtroom to try to discern the mood of the judge and the other participants. Every shrug, every bowed head, they interpreted to mean I was going to finally win the day. When five o'clock came, we left. We congratulated each other on the likelihood of success and went home to await the order.

Which didn't come before the holiday as promised. It came 4 days after Christmas. Not only did they throw out

Lillith's contempt charges, my custodial time was downgraded from 50% to 25%. I would see my beloved Sprout every other weekend. My older daughter was mandated to go to reunification counseling with me, which she had already blown off, so I saw no reason she would go now. I was mandated to go to counseling because I "talked to myself." It's funny how things sometimes look different when taken out of context and put into writing by a judge who has no idea what was meant when Sprout told him that. I talked to myself when watching sports—specifically anything that had to do with my Chicago sports teams—and I was playing the sportscaster. It was kind of a joke between me and Sprout I thought, but the judge obviously wasn't listening with his heart and made it seem like I had a mental problem. And the stuff about Lillith not communicating with me on behalf of our children? It was thrown out. As if it never happened. Christmas was supposed to be the happiest time of the year, especially for kids. Not this year. Not for my Sprout, not for me certainly. Merry Christmas.

INDIANAPOLIS
this is how it began

2003

My name is Sylvester Reyes. My friends call me Sly. My first name comes from my dad. He was a badass Chicago DJ back in the day, notorious 'cause he told it like it was through the music he chose to play and in particular, he loved kickass Sly and Family Stone. But that's another story. This one is mine. I have more than one reason for telling it. I'll start at the beginning.

Today, Tuesday, June 3, 2003 is the happiest day of my life. I'm 22 years old and I dreamed of being a father for three years now. Growing up in Indianapolis as a Puerto Rican kid in a city with no diversity, I yearned to start my own family and pass on my heritage. Create my own home. I have a decent job, a car, my own place. I'm very good at sports and play basketball and baseball whenever I get a chance. It's how I blow off steam and be myself. Work and sports. However, it's not optimum for meeting young women. And then, since there were only a handful of Puerto Rican families in Indianapolis in 2003, the odds of finding a

Puerto Rican woman who has the same dream as me are pretty slim, even if all I did *wasn't* just work and sports. So, I am VERY interested when a woman I play basketball with, Josephine, told me she has a niece she wants me to meet.

"Lilith," Josephine tells me. We're shooting some hoops, waiting for our games to start. "She's very pretty. She's 18 years old. She's a good girl."

This is the fantasy: I come home from work and a bunch of little kids swarm all over me, wrestling me to the ground. "Daddy, Daddy!" they would shout. All the pressures from work would fall away as I help them with their homework, play with them, toss some balls around probably—no, *undoubtedly* toss some balls around—until their mother would yell, "Time for dinner! Come on! You can't stay outside all night. Come *on*!" It's a pretty simple fantasy, right? A happy family. I would work my ass off to support everyone. That's no problem. I'm a very hard worker and if I had to work 20 jobs to support this, I would. I wanted a simple life. It's not as if I wanted to own a big multi-national company or be the first Latino president of the United States. I just wanted a happy family. When people said I was thinking too small, I would answer, "Having a happy family is the most important thing you can do!" And, I used to think, the easiest. It's almost like a right. The Chinese have a superstition that you can't let on to the gods what you want, what you value, because they take delight in denying you your heart's desire. And now, I think, they're right. While the rest of my life has been relatively easy, getting this one thing, a happy family, has proved to be the hardest thing I've ever done.

Lilith and I hung out a lot after we met. She wanted kids too and pretty soon she was pregnant. I immediately got a bigger apartment and put in for overtime. I was going to do this thing! Everything was falling into place, and I was happy for like 24 hours. One day after Lilith moved in, she moved back in with her mother. I joked with her that if she didn't like the ugly purple couches I bought for the living room, she could get something else, but she was just unhappy: just too young and immature to break away from her mother, who I soon learned had 5 other kids. I don't necessarily believe that you are doomed to repeat the mistakes of your parents, but it certainly gnawed at me. What if Lilith was like her mother?

I was locked out of everything: ultrasounds, doctor appointments. It was as if, "Okay, you did you part, now get lost." Like I was a freaking sperm donor or something.

This was certainly not part of my fantasy. But still, I hung in there, looking forward to reward of—what I learned, secondhand, I wasn't allowed in the ultrasound, remember?—our little girl. But I had to fight to stay in the picture. Lilith kept threatening to move to Puerto Rico and take the baby with her, so on a hunch, I made an appointment with a lawyer to find out what my rights were regarding my access to my daughter. I was ushered into his book-lined office by a skinny blond receptionist wearing an extremely tight sweater. The lawyer was a balding white guy, smoking a cigarette. I don't think he even looked at me.

"You got to go read the State of Indiana guidelines as it pertains to child custody," he said.

"What else?"

"That's it." He gave me the address of the law library in downtown Indianapolis. "It's pretty straight forward." He got up from behind the desk and saw me out, like making sure I left.

I paid the guy $1,500. Our conversation lasted four minutes. Before he closed the door on my back, I noticed his expensive Italian shoes. Naturally.

I read every book in the law library that pertained to child custody in the state of Indiana. Made a million copies of everything. As long as I paid child support, I would be granted 3 non-consecutive days a week, up to 2 hours each visit, to see my daughter. No problem there. I wanted my little girl to have everything. I sincerely believed, anyway, that once our girl was born, Lilith would soften. She was just young and scared and needed her mother.

Lilith's mother called me at work when Lilith went into labor. I took off early and rushed to the hospital, thinking I would be let in to see my little girl when she entered the world. I arrived at midnight.

"I'm sorry," the nurse at the command desk in the delivery room said, "Ms. Lilith has expressly said that only her mother is allowed in the delivery room."

"I'm the father," I said.

"Well, she's the mother, and she's allowed to have whoever she wants in there with her. Or not."

"Are you kidding me?" I asked. I certainly wasn't expecting this. "Her mother called me and told me to come."

"Her mother doesn't have permission to let you in," the

nurse said. She looked at me for the first time. "I'm sorry. There's a sofa over there where you can wait."

I nodded and lay down on the sofa. I was exhausted from work. But I couldn't sleep. I was too excited and angry, too, if I'm being honest. I had my rights. Although the State of Indiana didn't say anything about fathers being allowed to see the birth of their children. You would just assume that was something a father would be granted, right? Little did I know that this was just the beginning of the list of things I could no longer take for granted.

I was able to nod off a little, although the sofa was extremely uncomfortable, and my neck was killing me from sleeping at an impossible angle. I got up, rubbed it, and squinted down the hall to the Coke machine. A big analog clock on the wall informed me I had been asleep exactly fifteen minutes. It was going to be a long night.

The nurse that I talked to originally came by with a plate of cake and set it on the end table next to me. "One of the nurses is having a birthday," she said.

"Thanks."

She sat down next to me. "I'll let you know when it's getting close."

"Is it? Close?"

"Probably not. She's not dilated enough yet." She reached in her pocket and pulled out a plastic fork, stabbing it in the cake, then leaned in and whispered, "She's a bitch. You almost never have a father being apart from their child being born." She motioned to the cake and smiled. "You must be starved." Her hand brushed my knee.

I felt a familiar tingle. Here's the thing I haven't told you. I'm extremely attractive to women. I'm handsome, sure, and I hit the gym 5 days a week minimum. So, I look good, yeah. Add a job to the mix and bingo. Plus, the thing I have learned since becoming a father is that women are attracted to men who love their children. I wouldn't recommend having one just to get pussy, but if you happen to have one, and you happen to be crazy about the kid, it's an ace. It's like women can see that you're kind and responsible, and I think most women yearn to be treated kindly because most men are assholes in that regard. Of course, I have since learned that works both ways. Men do not have a monopoly on being assholes by any means.

I grabbed the fork and gobbled down the cake. "Good," I said through a mouthful.

She smiled and got up. "I'll check on you later. Let me know how it's going. Let me know if you need anything. Anything at all."

I walked to the vending machine and put in five dollars for a Coke. Five dollars! Between that and the sugary birthday cake, I was wired. I started walking down the hall, swigging the Coke, listening to muffled screams and moans coming from three different rooms. I froze. Lilith was in one of these rooms having my kid. I tried to see if I could tell the difference in the screams, but here's the thing: women screaming in childbirth all sound basically the same. Loud and in pain.

For a moment, I thought I could hear some Spanish being spoken in one room and I pivoted to sneak a peek—is that

Lilith?—when a firm hand grabbed me from behind.

"She isn't allowing visitors," the nurse, a different nurse, said.

"Her mother is in there," I said. "I'm the father."

"She specifically said she didn't want you."

"Don't I have any rights?" I asked. I was tired and wired and my censors were off. Up until this point I was trying to be polite so I would get my way, so they would see I wasn't a threat. What did Lilith tell them, anyway? Obviously now I had nothing to lose.

The nurse had taken my arm and was wheeling me around. "What do you mean, rights?"

"I mean, father's rights."

"I don't know what you're talking about young man, but unless she gives permission to allow you in, you're not going in."

She marched me back to my sofa, where someone else was now sitting. I sat in the chair. Looked at the clock. Ten minutes had gone by. Looked at the man who took my place on the sofa. He was calmly reading a book.

"Is this your first?" I asked him.

"Second," he said. "It doesn't get easier. The waiting. Nothing you can do except listen as they curse you out." He laughed. "You?"

"My first. But I want at least five." I was trying to picture how many little kids it would take to wrestle me to the ground when I got out of work. Four maybe. Five to be safe.

"I didn't really want any. But she did, so what can I do? I just work extra shifts to get out of the house."

The nurse who had shielded me from Lilith's room came back and beckoned to the man. "You can go in now."

He was a couple steps away from me when he turned around and yelled back, "Good Luck! Five!" He laughed. "You're crazy."

The tiny fraternity of men who want to be dads. With all the guys who fly off when they learn their girl is pregnant, you would think that I would be a cherished commodity. Instead, I'm in the hall like they found out I have leprosy.

I move to the sofa and fall into a deep sleep. I have this dream where I am surrounded by babies. All kinds of babies: black, brown, yellow, red, white. Screaming babies. I'm a DJ on weekends and if there is one thing I know, it's how to work a screaming crowd. In my dream, I put some vinyl on the turntable, 80s rock, some 90s and start to spin tunes. The babies, who could hardly crawl, are up and dancing, laughing, having a helluva good time. The lights are flashing, everyone dancing, but in the middle of all the happy noise, one baby is still screaming.

"It's okay!" I yell, "I'm here! What do you want to hear? I'll play it for you? Anything you want. I'm here."

"Mr. Reyes." Someone is shaking my arm, and I get up. "Mr. Reyes, get up. You have a baby girl."

She leads me to the nursery where they are cleaning the baby. My baby. Lilith is sleeping on the bed. She looks like hell. Well, she just had a baby. Her mother is gone. Figures. She's like a cat. When the aids finish cleaning the baby, they wrap it in swaddling and hand her to me. I hold her close and I see that little drops are falling on her face. I'm crying.

"Sorry, baby," I say. I start to convulse with emotion. "I'm your daddy. I'm your daddy."

"Are you okay?" the aid asks.

"Lady. That's what we're calling her. Lady." I'm completely out of control crying. I kiss her plump little cheeks. "She's all good, right?"

"She's perfect."

I hold her close to my chest and sob.

The aid holds out her arms. "I think I better put her in the bassinette." She takes Lady and another aid leads me out. "You better get some rest too," she says. "Are you okay? You were on that sofa for 32 hours."

"Am I allowed to stay?" I ask.

The aid looks uncomfortable. "There really is no place, since the mother doesn't want you in the room."

"Got it." I try to get another look at Lady. I think she looks like me. That gives me some rights, doesn't it? At least no one can deny paternity. The kid looks like me!

I find my car in the parking deck and put in the CD with the song "She's a Lady," the song Lilith and I were listening to when we decided to name our little girl, Lady. I am turned into a hopeless pile of mush. I cry uncontrollably. I don't know when I get to see Lady again. What the fuck. She's my kid.

Like I said, Tuesday, June 3, 2003. The happiest day of my life. I'm 22 and I dreamed of being a father for three years now.

And it's finally happened. She's here.

WHY LILITH?

So this is my story of trying to find a happy ever after with a woman who loved me and a bunch of little kids who could hardly wait to see me at the end of the day. It's also about why it seemed like it would never come.

Lots of people told me that my first mistake was wanting to have a family with only a Puerto Rican woman. That I would have had more luck in the romance department if I had cast a bigger net. But they have never felt the sting of being odd man out, like I was. I was always one of few Puerto Ricans in any group I was in. Can you blame me for wanting to have a family that looked like me? It seemed like an easy way to belong.

My family—that is my mother, father, me and my sister—left Chicago in 1994 or 1993 after the Bulls won their 3rd championship. Some people measure their lives by their relationships or jobs. I measure my life by sporting events. Anyway, after the Bulls won their 3rd championship, we moved to a little town: Martin, Tennessee. Ever hear of it? No, me either. I spent 7 months in a room alone, crying, suffering, didn't eat, didn't try to meet anyone. School was very difficult. Here I was coming from one of the most diverse cities in the world, finding myself in a very small town in the south. I was the first of my kind there. People didn't know what to think of me. They didn't teach different types of ethnicities or diversity, especially with there being so many different types of Hispanics. Even though my mom is white, my dad isn't. He has the afro with the curly hair so people didn't know what to make of it. They assumed all of us were the same, by that I mean, illegal Mexicans that came over 20 in a small trailer. I'm not trying to offend anybody, but this is the actual truth. I have facts that will back that up. Moving there in '93 was like going back in time.

So, they were still stuck, I'll give them a little leeway, and say they were still stuck in the 1940s and 1950s. That's how bad it was. I got bullied a lot. Got beat up. Spit on. Slapped in the face. Told, go back to where you came from, which was obviously Chicago, still part of the United States as these geniuses didn't know and only 6-8 hours north. Believe me, I would have loved to have gone back where I came from!

Schools there don't teach anything but what the old lazybutts tell them to teach. Information was never updated. It took me a long time to figure that out. I went to 7th and 8th grade and then on to high school. One friend, Franklin. He was a good-looking black guy. We went everywhere, did everything together. I picked up a couple of real friends along the way who are still friends, closer to me, I love them more than I love some of my family.

I have very little memory of my freshman year, I just know I was crying a lot, hiding from people. It was like I was in a mental coma for my whole freshman year. I still remember a lot of things people were telling me, like, "Go kill yourself." So, I took all that frustration and all that anger out in sports. Of course, if you're putting all that passion into something, you're going to get good at it and I did. I was so good, in fact, that I had a couple of opportunities to get scholarships to play baseball and basketball.

But, as soon as I was done with High School, the first thing out of my mouth is, "I'm going back to Chicago!" naturally, so I went back. I was there for about 6 months when some gang bangers stole a car and when they were running they smashed my car. I don't know if it was intentional or not. I remember my grandmother coming in the room and telling me in her best English accent possible, "They smashed your car," so I went out and checked it out. $10,000 in damages. It was totaled. I ended up going back to Tennessee where I got a job and worked for 2 years. Actually, it was in Kentucky. Across the state line. When I tell you that that's where racism hit me the hardest, I'm telling you the truth. You're talking about people who lived in the country for years, and they had all the stereotypes of Mexicans being soccer players, eating burritos, being illegal, crossing the border. I got it all. Here I am, a half Puerto Rican guy from the city of Chicago. Nobody can cope with that. I might as well have been from outer space. When we were able to listen to our radios at that job, I have some Spanish hip hop, or Spanish music and to them it was all just Mexican music. The stupidity was so bad, I kid you not, multiple people told me they didn't understand what the music was saying, even though it was 100% in English, but because it was sung by a PR or a Cuban, because it was rap and it was all in English, just because they had a New York accent—because that's where all the Dominicans, PR, Cuban rappers were from, they had the NY accent—and because people in the south don't know that NY accent, they would tell me the dumb shit like, "Can you change that? I don't know what they're saying." All I could do is throw my hands up and tuck that rage inside.

There were times when I got suspended, I had to be separated from people. They would make racial remarks and we would get 50/50 discipline. We would get the same, even though they were the ones making racial comments. Stereotyping, of course. It's obvious. I don't like the whole racial shit. That was the move to Tennessee.

Can you see why I wanted my own Puerto Rican family?

Two years of this bullshit and my mother's sister, Anne Marie, asked me to help her and her husband, Chris, move. They were both weirdos. Weird as hell. They were moving to Indianapolis. My aunt had gotten a job at a big insurance company. In fact, the headquarters of this insurance company was in Indianapolis. I thought, yeah, the Indiana Pacers played at the Field house, so I helped them move to an apartment complex called Heather Ridge at 38th and High School, and I stayed with them a couple of days. Chris was going to drive back to Tennessee to get the rest of the little stuff, so I was going to ride back with him. One day, as I was killing time waiting for Chris, I went to Target and buy a basketball and go down to the court. One night I heard a lot of people playing, so I go out to play and I'm like, " let me see what the city of Indianapolis has for basketball." They consider themselves to be kings in the sport of basketball, so I go out there, long story short, and there's this Puerto Rican girl playing, her name is Josephine, it's a weird name to say in English, and she was there with her nephew and her husband, his name was Louie, and so me and her played two on two with these two guys and she was doing all these funky dribbling and passing, and I was hitting everything. It was a nice hot night, and I'll never forget the show that I put on. People were going crazy. I couldn't miss, no matter what I did. So that night, she was like, "Yo! Nice playing with you." She used to play with the women's team in PR.

End of story, I think. I go back to Tennessee back to that shitty job. I'm living there for a while and it's unbearable. So, In April 2003, I finally quit that job, and I decided to move where my aunt was in Indianapolis. She told to come up, get a job, stay with her. So, exactly 2 years, so October of 2002, 2 years to that day, I moved to Indianapolis. I'm working odd jobs. Staying with my aunt. I sleep on a futon in a small bedroom they had.

So then, my dad comes up there. He's looking for a job. I'm waiting for him to get an apartment. After he gets an apartment, I live with my dad. I ended up getting a job at Carrier Heating and Cooling. At that plant of 1,500 there's one PR guy. I'm like, I gotta know him, but he saved me the trouble. He saw me at lunch and after seeing the PR flag on my sneakers, he said, in a very heavy accent, "Are you PR?" His name was Freddy. I told him, they call me by my middle name.

So, I said, "Hey, do you know about a Spanish lady who

plays basketball?"

He says, "You talking about Josephine." Apparently she was famous. He gave me her number. I was so excited I knew these people.

I got out of work, and I call Josephine and I said, "Hey do you remember me? I played basketball with you at Heather Ridge apartments last year?" and she said, "Omg, we got to meet up!"

So she invited me for dinner, and we shot basketball. I rode around with them for little bit. We became cool. Friends. Hanging out. Josephine had started the first Latino basketball league ever in the state of Indiana. Eleven Mexican teams, a lot of them played soccer, so they ran a million miles an hour. We're talking 10-15 players per team. So that's the number of Mexicans compared to Dominicans and PR. But there was one Dominican team and one PR team. I started playing on the team. I had some of the best basketball I ever played in my life. There was this one game where I scored 50, 60 points.

So, we're cool. And one day, after I'm living in Indianapolis for about a year, she tells me she has a niece she wants to introduce me to. She just turned 18.

"She's a good girl," Josephine tells me. She was living with her. In hindsight, I think she just wanted to get rid of her.

But still, I thought everything was finally going to turn out okay. That I had found my place in a world surrounded by people who were like me. Like family. That I could feel comfortable with. I said I would meet her.

LILITH SAYS, "I WANT MY MOMMY"

Lillith and I had immediate attraction, and she got pregnant right away. I was so ecstatic. I put in for overtime at my job so I could make more money, and we could get our home, our lives, established. I got an apartment. In my imagination I could already smell dinner cooking, and I could hear the kids screaming for me when I walked in the door.

However, I found out she couldn't cook, so my idea of having good PR food was thrown out the window. But, hey, there's lots of places that make that stuff so no big deal. I also found out she didn't like cleaning, so I had to do everything, but again, no big deal. I was willing to do everything to create the life I envisioned.

I bought new furniture and stuff for the kitchen. I bought us a purple couch, brand new. Purple was both our favorite colors. I was so young and stupid I thought that having the same favorite color was enough to base a life on. That idea held for about 5 months to when Lillith moved into the apartment. She was there for 24 hours. I came home from a 10-hour shift, and she was lying on the purple couch.

"I want to go back to my mother's," she said.

I'm like, "Why? What happened?"

"I'm just like, bored," she said.

It turned out that she couldn't handle being by herself.

She was too young and immature. I kind of got it. She was only 18 years old, five months pregnant, and I guess it was kind of boring just sitting in an apartment all day waiting for me to come home.

That was early December. At the end of December, stuff with my parents came down. My dad was a DJ, pretty famous one actually, and my mom was getting bored sitting at home, too, it turns out and was having her own issues. My sister got in the middle of it, took my dad's side, and my mom ended up leaving. I don't talk to my sister to this day. Anyway, my mom moved into my apartment. It was okay. I got along with my mom, and she could cook and clean and I was looking forward to Lillith having our kid, even if she wasn't living with me. My parents' divorce was final in 2005.

But what I was saying before? That what should have been the easiest thing in the world—having a family—was for some reason the hardest thing for me to achieve? Yeah. I came home one day and the apartment was empty. Everything was gone. My mom took it all. She found a boyfriend and was living with him now. I guess she got him to take it. But so what? It didn't matter. I was making good money, so I just went out and got new things. That was that.

I was talking to Lillith now and then on the phone and so I thought everything was cool. That I would be with her when she delivered, but I already told you how that went down. I ended up sleeping on the couch in the hallway of the hospital.

But, what I wasn't expecting was that I wouldn't be allowed to see my daughter after she left the hospital. I hadn't realized that Lillith's family was psycho. Lady was a week old when I went to her mother's apartment. Did I mention that Lillith's mother had 5 other children from different fathers? They all still lived with her, in her tiny apartment in an apartment complex. That's what was waiting for me when I went to see Lady when she was a little over a week old. I was so excited I was shaking.

They let me in, and Lillith brought Lady downstairs for me to visit then went back upstairs, and I was there admiring Lady for a few minutes when all the demons—that is the mother and siblings—came at me. I had my phone out, taking a few pictures. I didn't understand Spanish at that time, so I didn't know what triggered them. Her sister was in my face, slapping me. Her mother took my phone. Her mom threw the phone at me. Lillith came downstairs to take Lady away. And I ran the hell out of there.

I slammed the door, and everybody came running out after me. I took off from the complex. I remember at some point, I turned around and fought back. But when I looked up at the 2d floor window, hoping to see Lillith and the baby, no one was there.

It was just as well I didn't see the baby, because I just had this image of her looking at me and I didn't want her first memory of me to be fighting a bunch of these people. Anyway, I couldn't hit any of them, they were kids. Her brothers were teenagers, 12 and 13 years old. And Lillith and her mother? I couldn't hit women. This was the violent lifestyle they were used to, but I couldn't hit a female, and I couldn't smack a kid. I decided to go back to the entrance and call the cops. But first, I look at my car. Someone had key scratched both sides of it, and the rock they used was still by the driver's door.

It took the cops two hours to come. Naturally. Help comes slow to black and brown people, no matter what side of the law they're on. The cops escorted me back and gave me a police report that said that I would need an escort to go back in there, so now I couldn't see my daughter until we went to court.

That was in April. In August we were before the judge who said that Lillith had to meet me at a neutral location, because her family had created a hostile environment. We decided on the fire house because it was close to her. That's where she would hand over Lady to me. But the first time I go there, she never showed up. I kept texting her for an hour, "Where's my child? Bring me my child" and she refused to bring Lady telling me I had to go to her. So, I went over there, she brought my daughter out and all the neighbors were watching me. I put my daughter in the car seat, it was like, are they really going to do something when I'm putting a three-month-old baby in my car? But the messages I was receiving from Lillth were, "Can we please talk? Can we do this together?" blah blah blah. And then she ended coming with Lady when I was picking her up because supposedly she was breast feeding. So, what I did was, I would bring Lady to my house for these visits and leave Lillith outside. She had to stay outside. I would lock the door. She either had to sit on the stairs in the hallway in the apartment or wait outside in the car. For two hours. Then I would take her and Lady back. Even through all of that, I still brought her with me in case Lady got hungry, which a couple of times she did, so I took her outside and said, "Can you feed her?" I said I still have 2 hours so if you're with her for 20 minutes, I'm going to add 20 minutes to my time. It was very pathetic that I had to do that. Anyway, there were some hot days, and being the person I am, I allowed Lillith to come into my house where there was air conditioning because in Indiana sometimes it was 90 some degrees outside. And obviously I wasn't going to leave her outside or in the hallways, which was hotter. I just wanted to add this because no matter what she did to me I stood up and allowed her to stay in my house and I wasn't able to enjoy my 2 hours, like I was supposed to have.

Still, even though we had these altercations, and her family was still hostile to me for God knows what reason, Lillith's family are my family I think. So, when her mom got evicted from her apartment—6 people that management didn't know about were living a 2 bedroom apartment—they came and stayed with me. I forgot to mention that after the attack, I moved into my dad's house. It was a bilevel home, and I was living downstairs. I had 2 bedrooms, a bathroom and a living room. I gave them 3 days to stay with me and I told them by Monday they had to leave. But they didn't make it to Monday. My dad came home Friday night, yelling, this is no damned hotel, so they had leave the next morning and went to live with another of Lilith's aunts who lived in a smaller 2 bedroom, so now it was 7 people living in a small 2-bedroom apartment. Whatever. It seemed like they were used to it.

The irony to me is that later, when I went for custody of my kids, the court demanded that each kid have their own bedroom. It's not a standard that most people can meet and it's certainly not normal for regular families to have separate bedrooms for each of their kids.

Anyway, this went on for a while. Occasionally the whole team moved in with me, three times over the course of several years, the last time was when Lillith's uncle, her mother's brother, sent the whole crew Amtrak tickets to New Bedford, Massachusetts.

I could feel my dream evaporating. Lady getting further and further away from me.

I told Lilith, "If you take Lady across state line, I will get you for kidnapping." Which I was certainly in my rights to do, but then we were sort of forced to live together at that point. Her mom left, and that started 9 years of me taking care of her and Lady.

THE WAR OF THE ROSES

There's probably no better recipe for unhappiness than having a fixed idea of what happiness should look like. That would make a great meme, wouldn't it? Because it's true. I spent a lot of time, too much time really, trying to force my idea of happiness, which I thought was normal and regular, into an irregular reality.

I thought that once Lilith and I were forced to live together so we could both see Lady, that our problems would disappear. But it was only the beginning.

I was working three jobs—none of them high paying—to try to make a life for the three of us. It wasn't much, minimum wage being as they say, minimum. And I kept asking Lillith to pitch in, get some work. At least, I thought, she could do some of the housework and cooking. For whatever reason, she didn't. She stayed home watching television most of the time. I don't know what she did with the rest of her time.

Our second child, Sprout, was born in 2010. For some misguided reason, I thought that would change things.

2011 TRYING TO MAKE IT WORK

And this is where it gets REALLY crazy...

We were living in Indiana, and I already told you about a lot of the racism there. So, naturally, since Lillith's family lived in Massachusetts, and she wasn't working or doing anything else that required her presence, I told Lillith I would drive her and the girls there. By the way, Indiana is a good 14-hour trip from Massachusetts. Forget the fact that I had to take off work to do this.

Anyway, on the way back I decided to take a break and stop in Catasauqua, Pennsylvania where I had some relatives I had just discovered. I liked Catasauqua because a big Latino population lives there, and I felt at home. I also realized there was a demand for my DJ skills.

At the end of the summer, I picked up my family in Massachusetts and drove them back to Indiana. I guess I shouldn't have been surprised when I got back that I found out that my biggest job had fired me. I took too much time off. Most of the money I was making was going into rent, so of course we couldn't afford our apartment and had to leave. We ended up moving in with my friend Danny, a fellow DJ, and his wife and two daughters. Needless to say, it wasn't a comfortable living arrangement, and I started spending 4 to 5 hours at the gym to escape, and pretty soon Danny started joining me.

I decided that it wasn't a good environment for us, and we agreed to move to Pennsylvania. In my mind, Pennsylvania was heaven, because it had so much diversity. I moved first. Got a job, got an apartment, then I moved the family. We lived in Hidden Village, which was near the airport. We were there for 3 months, and it became clear that Lillith wasn't going to get a job or help with the cooking and cleaning. She wasn't going to do anything, and we needed the money. We got evicted, naturally.

Her mom came and took her and the girls back to Massachusetts. Lady was screaming that she didn't want me to go. Sprout was too little to know what was happening, but she was crying too. Me, too. I was crying. I couldn't bear to not see my kids every day.

But I forged ahead with the move to Pennsylvania. I got enough money to get a small apartment in Catasauqua with my uncle's help. That was how I met my uncle's childhood friend, Luke. It would be kind to say that Luke was a snake. I admit that things weren't great with Lillith and me, but maybe the whole fight over the kids wouldn't have happened if Luke hadn't been such a desperate ass.

Here's how it happened. I got DJ gigs and when I started deejaying, Luke started coming out with his girlfriend Milagros, a Dominican girl. He drank lots of beer and left early. Milagros ended up leaving him. It was pretty clear he had a problem with alcohol. But it wasn't my problem, right?

I had my own place and was spending a little time on social media. I noticed that every time I posted pictures of my kids he liked them. He was acting like he was my big special friend. He even offered to have me moved into his trailer with him. I refused, not because I didn't like him, but because it was far from where I worked and most of all, because I wanted to get a place for me and Lillith and the kids.

Which I did. I found a great apartment for me and Lillith, Lady, and Sprout. I was so happy to tell Lillith that we could all move in that I called her immediately. And this is what she said, "It's too late for that."

I almost dropped the phone. It had only been three weeks. What was she talking about? What could have happened in three weeks?

My cousin, Maryann, came into the room then and said, "You got to see this." It was a Facebook post of a live chat between Lillith and Luke. Something was going on between them.

Maryann knew Milagros and told me Milagros said she didn't want Luke to be around her girls because of his excessive drinking.

I called Lillith and said, "If you go in this guy's house, if you touch him. I'll never take you back." Then I broke down and cried for a couple of hours.

How could Luke have inserted himself into my family? He must have been painting her one hell of a pretty picture. I wondered if Lillith knew that the trailer he lived in and was promoting as some kind of fucking castle was really small.

I retreated into music, thinking that DJing would make me happy. I figured that was the easiest way to deal with my life. But I also knew I had to be with Lillith to be with my kids, and while maybe I didn't really care that she was with Luke—hell, he could take her off my hands—I knew that I had to be with Lillith to see them at least half time.

I slept in my car. I stopped talking to my uncle and aunt Fiona who was advising Lillith on how to get child support from me. Yeah, soon enough, my wages were being garnished for $200 a week. Yeah, Domestics knows how to hustle when they can screw a father. Lillith's sister, Cecilia, is calling me and told me that Lillith and Luke were on the phone 24/7, they were falling asleep on the phone. (Years later I am still paying off that $2,000 Verizon bill. Actually, I stopped paying, because WTF, right? But it wrecked my credit.) This is October 2013.

I'm going through all this, going crazy. My life had suddenly turned from just trying to provide for my family to trying to provide for my family and stay alive myself.

I have all of Lillith's stuff in storage. And when I move into the apartment, I tell Lillith you need to get your stuff. Somewhere in my heart, I think she'll see me and change her mind and come back. Well, you can guess how that goes.

She tells me she's moving to Pennsylvania, yes, but with Luke. With Luke who can't drive out of state because of his DUIs. The kids are 8 and 3 at the time. I guess Luke got someone to drive the van to Massachusetts and pick up Lillith and the girls. Lillith grabs whatever she can from her mom's and leaves, driving back to Pennsylvania and moving into Luke's trailer without meeting him in person.

So, here I was. My kids are living in a tiny trailer in

Breiningsville. I'm getting $200 a week taken from my paycheck for child support and nothing is established about me being able to see my kids regularly.

Eventually, Lillith agrees that I can take the kids for an afternoon, but when I pick them up and hug Lady, she wouldn't hug me back. I keep asking her what's wrong and she won't even look me in the eyes in the rear-view mirror. Finally, she blurts out, "You were never there for us. You never were there for us!"

I wanted to scream, "Who told you this! I did everything I could!" But how do you explain this to an eight-year-old? In just a few weeks, someone—guess who?—was filling her head with the idea that I was slacking off somewhere.

Somewhere in the back of my mind, I kept thinking that Lillith would come around and be sane. I knew that she was obsessed with me, and once when I picked up the kids and we stopped off at a diner to have something to eat, Lady started crying hysterically saying Lillith fell on the floor and was screaming that she "missed Daddy."

I couldn't handle life not seeing my daughters every day like I used to. So, I created a customized court order, detailing how I could see my kids. I didn't have regular hours at Coca Cola, so I couldn't just put in for regular hours. As if you didn't know, everything in life costs, and I had to pay 260 dollars for the first filing fee.

In Pennsylvania, before you go to court you go to a mediation hearing. Donald Quarier was my lawyer. He was famous, and even has a street named after him in Easton, so

I expected to get what I wanted. The headmaster runs the mediation session, and I told her I wanted them on Wednesdays and three weekends a month.

I was living with my friend Gloria then. She was a wedding photographer that I met at a DJ gig and we became best friends. She had my back. I thought that if they knew Gloria was living with me it would work against me, so I asked her to live with her sister when the girls came. She was doing research on father's rights for me and showed me what was happening on social media: I was getting blasted as a deadbeat by Lillith. She was telling everyone I was unstable, just moving around all the time. She seemed to have forgotten that I actually sold the washer and dryer to buy her a laptop so she could go back to school. That I paid for her to go to cosmetology school, which she dropped out of. But she kept up the bashing for everyone to see.

Worse, she was posting obscene pictures of me. They were so bad, I can't even tell you what they were. But what was the worst? It was a picture of Lillith laying in bed with her phone and Lady and Sprout were poking their heads around the open door. Lillith held her phone up and a little bubble over her head said, "Want to talk to Daddy?" The bubble over Sprout's head said, "Who?" and the bubble over Lady's head said, "Fuck no." God that hurt. People who didn't even know me were commenting on it. Aunt Fiona puts her ugly beak in too. When I first saw that, my mom was with me and I broke down, literally. She had to throw a blanket over me and wrestle me to ground, saying "We will get through this."

I show all this stuff to the mediator who says, "We get that stuff all the time. Cut it out. Both of you."

I got every other weekend. Same as everyone.

This was in December 2013. I wasn't looking forward to the holidays. I had never spent them without my kids. New Years Eve, it was frozen outside. A blizzard. It was my first real winter in Pennsylvania. Me and Gloria were looking through the back door, trying to encourage each other. "We got this," we said. We hugged. I had my first bout of depression then. I felt myself sinking into a black hole. Gloria honestly thought that everything was okay, and she kept toasting the new year and how well I was doing, but a voice inside me told me that a war was starting.

TRUE LOVE ENTERS THE PICTURE: BIANCA
2014

Of course, I did all the driving all while having child support taken out of my check. I was making 13 bucks an hour, and I had $250 taken out of each paycheck. Do the math, and try living on that. But I tried to make it work the best I could. I got season passes to Dorney Park, and I made sure I got the girls something from McDonald's, even if it was a sandwich and small Coke. And life goes on. I'm getting my kids according to the court order and of course it's cold outside so me, Lady, and Sprout are in my new apartment where we play video games, and later I take them out to eat. They sleep over. In their own room of course.

Usually, I'm living life by myself. Doing little DJ gigs here and there. My name is starting to take off at this point. My life is normally quiet, but I am starting to meet some people. Through Gloria I met Brenda and from there I met DJ Lexus who kind of took me under his wing. He had a radio show called Hot 101. I made a couple guests appearances on their radio show/podcast. I met Ginger and Danny, another couple. So, I'm meeting quite a few people and thinking everything is good. And my name is taking off through talking, through being friends on Facebook with Brenda who had a lot of friends because she worked at Cedarbrook.

One of her friends was a woman named Bianca. Her name was Biscochito on Facebook. Biscochito means cupcake in English. Cute, right? I always see her liking and commenting, so I snooped around and did my due diligence "as a DJ" as I told myself, adding people who were mutual friends of my friends and so forth. So, I became Bianca's friend. At the time I could tell she was in the end stages of her relationship, and I would message her once in a while. One night, I guess Bianca was intoxicated when I messaged her, and we started talking. Nothing flirty but, honestly, I was very attracted to her. A Dominican girl with blonde hair. Physical attributes that were what I like. Umm. But I didn't force the issue. We just started talking on Facebook, and she started liking pictures of me at the gym and me with my kids. And then, on Valentine's Day, she sarcastically posts a picture of her front porch, and she adds these stickers of roses, chocolates, and a stuffed animal. I can take a hint! But I still didn't want to force it remembering she was going in for surgery soon, and I asked if I could bring a get-well bag to her house. I would just leave it on her front porch. That way, it's not an awkward visit. I wanted to leave her something for Valentine's Day, too, so I asked her do you mind if I drop something off? She says OK, that's fine and gave me her address. Come to find out that I lived right down the street from her, I had no idea. Remember, Bianca and I never met in person, so we're both taking a chance.

I took the picture that she posted, the sarcastic picture with the stickers of the flowers, chocolates, and stuffed animal, then I bought those same flowers, chocolates, and stuffed animal and left them on her front porch. And took a picture of it. I was really pleased with myself. It looked exactly like her photo.

Later on that night she messaged me and said, "Did you leave something at my front door?"

I matched my picture with her picture, sent it, and said, "Was I close enough?"

I think she might have been crying. She said, "That's the sweetest thing anybody's ever done for me."

Her kids ended up taking the chocolate, of course. Because that's what kids do. I think I was crying a little too. I had all this love to give, and I was holding all these sweet things inside, because I didn't do it for the nine years that I was living with Lillith. I wanted to let it out.

So, I was really interested in dating her, and I was persistent. I caught her attention. So then about 2-3 weeks after that it was March of 2014. It turned out, that's when her surgery was scheduled, so I used that as an excuse to get closer. Brenda, Gloria, Bianca and Ronna were all friends and they were getting together for a dinner. I told Brenda, "Put in a good word for me."

I'm trying to meet Bianca in person without seeming too anxious. I'm trying to see what we have in common. And I come to find out, I have a dog. She has a dog. We use the same bank, which I lived right next to. And like I said, she lived about 2 blocks away. A coincidence I decided to make work for me.

So, one Friday night I'm going to the club, Pitchers. I had a nice blue suit on. It was when Pitchers was still open on

Union Blvd. And I was gonna go meet Gloria and a couple of friends at Pitchers, because, they said, it was time for me to get out, start networking, and putting my name out there. So, as casually as I could, I told Bianca, "Hey, I'm going to the bank. Would it be possible to say hi at the parking lot at the bank?"

I was so relieved she said yes. I'm waiting nervously in the parking lot, and she pulls up in her van. Here's the thing: When I see her, I was lost for words. She looked more beautiful in person than she did in social media pictures.

The only thing that came out of my mouth was, "Hey you" and she said, "Hey you." Brilliant, right? But we started chatting and blah blah blah and eventually I tore myself away and went to the club, and all I was thinking about was her and how I wanted to see her again. I didn't want to text her right away because of the nerves and whatever.

So, her surgery happened that week. When she got out of the hospital I texted her, "Hey, I wanna stop by. I have something for you." It was just a get-well bag with a teddy bear, some flowers, and some of her favorite snacks.

"Come on over," she says.

She meets me outside. One of her four boys runs out of the house to see what she's doing—it's dark out—and he called me "Delvis" which is the guy that Bianca was trying to break with.

And I was like, "Oh, the famous Delvis."

"I'm sorry," she says. "He comes by once in a great while and my son knows him."

But it was cool. After that, me and Bianca started hanging

out. She invited me over to her apartment, and I did the whole romantic thing with candles and some jazz playing on the phone. We got together and it was a full head of steam from there and we took off. I was in love for the first time in my life.

And I was happy. I started meeting more people, too. Mostly through Brenda and DJ Lexus. And so one night I went out to Lynx across from Dorney Park just to hang out, and I was introduced to Bill and Dawn. They were very friendly and Bill pulls me aside and asks me if I would be interested in a DJ gig.

"DJ Lexus is moving to Florida and you're funny and good looking," he tells me. "I think you'd be a hit."

I wasn't sure what being good looking had to do with being a good DJ, but I agree and he says, "Just so you know what to expect, this is a private swingers event. First Sunday of every month." Oh.

And I was like, "Yeah, sure." Because I felt I was professional enough to handle something like a swinger's event even though I had never been to one.

A couple of the people who participated in these events came out to the Lynx then. I was cracking jokes on the mic and being generally entertaining and I was in great shape and they fell in love with me right away. So, I became their DJ.

My first swingers event was in May. I told Bianca, "Hey, I've never done anything like this. Would you come keep me company?"

It was risky to ask, but she was a good sport. She showed up in a mask, it was 2014, and she didn't judge me. She sat next to me, and we both had butterflies giving each other the side eye. It's funny, thinking about it now. But that's the first time I experienced actually being in love with somebody. I knew it was love because I couldn't stand being without her. I just hated being without her. And it was my first time being with somebody that had their own house, had an education, had a job, took care of her kids on her own, paid her own bills, bought groceries, cooked, put gas in her car, everything. Very, very strong, independent woman. I never had that. I never really had the *opportunity* to have that because I was in a relationship for nine years, dealing with somebody who did nothing. I had to do everything. I sacrificed almost a decade of my life to be with my kids, and I've realized that I put my kids over my personal happiness and now I only have them every other weekend and every other Wednesday, such bullshit, but still I figured, hey, I have my kids, I have my job. It's time to settle down.

What was crazy is that Bianca's birthday was July 19th and mine was the 20th, so we're already making plans. We're all going to go on vacation and I was happy.

I remember me and Bianca's first date. Are you tired of me talking about her? Ha. I could talk about her all day. Our first date, we dressed up really nice and went to the Olive Garden and sat down and we just enjoyed each other 's company. No drama. I didn't tell her anything about my court appearances cause I didn't want drama. When we left, I really looked at her. She wore this green shirt, jeans, and heels. I never imagined in my lifetime that I would be with somebody who looks like this. I wanted to show her off, so

I suggested we go see Gloria, the photographer and Brenda the cake decorator. Brenda's husband was there too. They were playing freestyle music. I guess they know all the big freestyle hits, trying to set the vibe to make me feel comfortable. A couple of other people were there.

But something was off. Brenda had a very beautiful house, and I was wondering how she could afford a house like that when her husband worked at Coca-Cola with me making $13 an hour. I didn't ask any questions, but it was odd. Well, I did ask her, "How come you don't have any pictures or anything up?" and she looked a little frantic. I think that's when I started to think that maybe things weren't quite right here. Like I said, I just wanted to settle down and have a normal life and I wasn't in the market for weird, so I said, "Brenda, I'm just gonna do these last two gigs and that's it. It's becoming a lot with my new job and I just want to focus on that because there was good money to be made there."

Brenda and I had two gigs planned that were already booked and paid for. Brenda paid me upfront, $400 for one event and $500 for the other. We didn't have a contract or anything. But still, I would honor my commitment.

"And," I said, "I just want to enjoy my relationship and my kids and stuff."

She didn't respond, so I just left and that was it. There was nothing to say after that. I thought she understood. This was in March. I didn't know at the time how deeply disturbed she was. She took the fact that I didn't want to work with her very personally. And she took my questioning of her minimalist house as a threat to some kind of secret she was carrying.

Brenda took her crew, the people who were subcontractors to her on wedding gigs, on a cruise and she indoctrinated everyone with her how much of a pervert I was. It must have been that, because when they came back, that's when everything started to become undone.

In April, Lillith and I had another mediation. Lady didn't want to come over anymore and the arguments were getting out of control.

It started with the accusations that Bianca's boys were exposing themselves to Lady and Sprout. Bianca's four-year-old, five-year-old, seven-year-old having their privates out in front of Sprout, who was then three or four? When I questioned her, she didn't know anything about that. Bianca wasn't there, she was out with me. Bianca's mom was taking care of the boys. That's how little kids are, they're oblivious to stuff like that. So, that was the first accusation. It came months later. After the brainwashing took place, filling Lady's head with all this stuff. Do you think it's just a coincidence that Donna, Lillith's neighbor was a retired employee of Children and Youth? I'm not stupid. Anyone with half a brain can see that Donna was giving Lillith and Lady tips. If you don't wanna go over there, just say that the boys did this to you. That was 100% obvious because Donna was one of the people that hid behind the car, videotaping me every time I went and picked up and dropped off.

Of course, Lady stopped coming over. Even after months of counseling with Lady and Sprout, I couldn't bring them back to the house. I had to stay out. So on Saturdays I would drive to Breinigsville, stay out all day trying to find somewhere to go, something to do, spending money. Gas money, food money because I couldn't bring them back to the house. So that went on for months. So whatever little DJ money, I was making 150 bucks a night for a whole DJ gig at a club. I was using that just to stay out and about with Sprout because I couldn't bring her back to the house.

This didn't just affect me and the girls, though, it affected Bianca too. Children and Youth came over, interrogated Bianca's kids asked them questions. Bianca comes home and the look in her eye as a mother seeing her kids interrogated over such sick accusations. When I look back at it now, I can see that Bianca was thinking, Why is this monster asking my kids these questions. Get out of my house. Then she turns her rage to Lillith, as in "I want to kill her. I wanna mess her up." But then at the end of the day, she was thinking, "I would never be in this mess if I wasn't with this guy." That started the downward spiral of what was to be a beautiful, perfect, lifelong marriage, happy couple, happy life.

Not being able to see Lady was killing me. I was crying in the showers and sitting in my car at night crying. I lost a lot of sleep. The trauma of that was the beginning of my depression, leading up the evil side of me comes out a few years later. But the emotional trauma I was suffering was unbearable. So having to sit in a small mediation room with my lawyer, Lillith, and her lawyer was hell. Lilith doesn't let anybody finish talking. She's making faces, little smirks. And of course, they don't say anything to her, but I'm constantly being told that I need to cool down. If I snap or blow up, "you'll never see your kids again and you're gonna lose everything you've been fighting for."

Anyway, no matter what proof I showed the mediator, screen shots, text messages of her bashing me, text messages from my daughter saying she isn't coming over, etc. No matter what I said about Lillith not abiding by the court order, and I haven't seen my daughter on my weekends as the court order clearly states, AND children aren't supposed to get involved with the exchange of custody, and I have my nine-year-old calling me, telling me she's not coming with me…they don't do anything. And then I'm supposed to stay calm, not supposed to yell at her, but I'm getting frustrated.

Mediation was a complete waste of time. I got no justice out of it. The headmaster didn't like me for some reason. She was very aggressive towards me.

Because me and Bianca were dating, Lady didn't wanna come over. I don't know how much easier we could have made it because even without my knowledge, Bianca reached out to Lillith and told her, "Hey, your girls are beautiful and I wish I could have had daughters," blah blah blah, and "If you ever need anything, let me know if you ever need me to drive out there and pick them up, here's my phone number, call me. I don't mind. Maybe we can get together one day." And Lillith completely ignores it.

Lady stopped coming around entirely. She said she didn't want to come to the house because she didn't like Bianca. I wanted another hearing. But I have to pay my lawyer for these hearings. One thousand dollars, then one thousand

and five hundred dollars. Then two thousand dollars. The price kept going up because these lawyers know that idiots like me are not going to stop fighting. So, all they did was take whatever money I had. I was borrowing money from people. It just got to the point where it was embarrassing.

It was getting tense picking up and dropping off Sprout, too. Luke was out there, constantly causing tension standing out there with his chest out, yelling "this is my house" and I was never able to have a peaceful pickup or drop off. So, I filed mediation just to emphasize that I didn't want any communication with Lillith unless it's through text or e-mail, because they keep calling me, threatening me, yelling at me, cursing at me, and then hanging up the phone on me. And when I call back, I'm like a maniac going crazy. Surprise.

I would get so mad, I had to leave late at night from Bianca's house instead of eating dinner, taking a shower and going to bed. Instead, I'd leave the house at 9:00, go somewhere and sit in the parking lot, trying to catch my breath. My head is pounding and I'm punching the steering wheel. I would come back around midnight and wake up at 4:00 AM and be at work by five or five thirty.

It was Luke that was causing this tension. I even wrote in the custodial order that he should not be allowed to be around during pickup and drop off. They gave that to me. They *awarded* that to me. But do you think they followed those rules, that court order? Hell no. It went on and on and it went on, so at this point, I filed for physical custody of both of my kids. Giving weekend visitations to the mother. The plan was we would agree to 50/50.

Of course, that wasn't the case. Of course, they deny me that. And instead they give me this BS rule where I can no longer bring Bianca back to the house after the accusations of the kids. Excellent.

If Lillith wasn't vindictive enough already, she became worse. In June, I was 15 minutes late picking up Sprout. I texted saying I had a meeting at work and would be a little late, but she didn't respond and when I got to her house and texted her, "I'm here," she made me wait and I hardly got to spend any time with Sprout.

That should have been contempt, right? Violation of the court order written by a judge in the Commonwealth of Pennsylvania? And she's clearly breaking the order, and I'm showing all this proof. And of course, nothing was done. No concern. Nothing. But, of course, I'm getting yelled at.

In July, DJ Lexus, who had a radio show on Hot 101.net invited Ahria and her show, "Talk to Me." It was basically a gossip shop. Guess who was a guest? Brenda. And Lilith. Don't ask me how, but Lilith and Brenda became big pals with the common denominator being trying to bring me down. Everyone was on the show bashing me, calling me names, a molester. A perv. Someone finally calls me up and says, "You better get on there, bro, and tell your side of the story." So, I call in. I try to stay calm and tell what I think is going on, when all of a sudden they put Lady on and she starts bashing me, too. I quietly click off. It was out there now. I was officially the bad guy and I didn't know what I had done except try to be a father to my girls.

So, a month later, in August, I filed again. This time my

petition for contempt stated Lilith's not allowed to keep me from seeing my kids. But she had someone else email and text me that I wouldn't see my kids until the August 18 hearing. She kept having Lady call me to tell me that she's not coming. And Lillith kept making plans for Lady on my time and without my consent, so I have to be the bad guy and tell her, "No, you're coming with me." She's turning me into the monster. Obviously she's brainwashing my child. And bribing her. I'm the one who has to tell her, "No, you can't be with your friends, because you're coming with me."

Lady started hating me. But I did get Sprout. I will say, there was no taking her away from me then.

I filed on August 4 for a hearing on August 18.

In the meantime…is this starting to sound like I'm making it up? Because sometimes it feels like it can't be real—Lillith files against me in an act of retaliation. She claims incidents are happening when I'm at work and the kids are with Bianca or Bianca's mom and the four boys. She says Lady is scared to go to Bianca's because Bianca's 8-year-old boy chased her with his privates out. And Sprout, who is 3 years old, is saying that she was forced to take a bubble bath with two of the younger boys. And she names them. Mind you, me and Bianca don't have a bathtub in our house. We have a stand-up shower. But no one bothers to ask me to verify. So, the case worker for children tells Lillith she needs to file for emergency custody. And I have to be there when the case is presented. I have to take a day off of work, which I need to work because all this child support is coming out of my pay. I can't be with my kids because I have a job, but I must be at home because the little boys are walking around with their penises out.

So, of course, we have to go to mediation. Lillith is making faces at me, laughing when nobody's looking. Of course, they don't say anything to her, but I have to sit there like a criminal with my hands folded. I can't even breathe, can't move, can't do anything. So yeah, I'm getting provoked. The mediator gets tired of it and she throws the case out and says, "You guys are going in front of the judge."

So here we go in front of Judge Liebman.

GOING ON A CRUISE AND GETTING MARRIED

2015

2015 was starting to look up. I was doing private gigs. I'm doing good at my job. I'm still a temp, still making 13 bucks an hour, but working a lot of overtime, doing my little private gigs for 200 bucks a pop. That was the biggest DJ gig I had at that point.

I was still seeing Sprout, but I had to figure out a way to get Lady back into my life. She was slowly coming around after the holidays. She didn't come in the house, but she came to hang out and wouldn't sleep over. The counselors were constantly telling Lillith, "She needs to be with her dad," so, me and Lady had a couple counseling sessions. Obviously Lady didn't tell her that Momma said this and Momma said that, and I couldn't sit in front of her and tell the counselor that Momma was a liar. I couldn't talk bad about her mother like that.

Anyway, after the counseling sessions, Lady starts coming around. I bought her a bike so she can have something to do when she comes over. And she starts coming over for a couple of hours every other weekend. I got Sunday. She would come over for about two or three hours. Mind you, I was doing all the driving cause step-dad had a drinking and driving problem and he kept losing his license. But I did whatever it took.

I started DJing at Bar with No Name in January and summer is coming. That's where the DJ Ivo name took off. I had to open social media back up to promote myself and right away I started blocking everybody so nobody could have access to me. And, apparently people don't have lives or anything better to do, because more fake Facebook pages are coming, but I'll get to that.

In the meantime, I'm rocking out. They love it. I get requested, and my name's blowing up. Then I get my first DJ paycheck from there, $350. And that was life changing for me because now I have extra money to go and waste on lawyers and file for mediations.

And then the Disney Cruise comes. I pursued this hoping it would bond our families. Both individually and together. I went to the courts, asked permission to take my daughters on the Disney cruise. Both of them. We have to clear it with Lillith. Do have any reason they can't go? And of course Mom wants to make herself look good because she doesn't want me to take my kids on vacation. She doesn't want me to be on a Disney cruise. She doesn't want her kids around me when I'm with another woman. Mind you, they're living in a trailer with Luke. But that's beside the point. So anyway. Disney Cruise is coming. I'm working overtime. I work 40 hours during the week. Couple nights work 12 hours, Saturday work 12 hours. Go home. Shower, change. Go DJ till two in the morning. Go home. Shower, change, sleep two hours. Wake up, work 12 hours, Go home. Go right to sleep on a Sunday night and do it all over again.

I saved up all this money to go on a Disney cruise. It was me, my mom, JJ Varna, Bianca and her four boys, her mom, her sister and her dad. So as all of us going, and of course me and Bianca had to pay for everybody. That shows you how much overtime and DJing I was doing just to raise money so we can go on a Disney Cruise. I'm not forcing Lady, but she's close with my mom, so she feels comfortable with her, and so she came.

So we leave for Florida, and her mom obviously knows. Because I had to ask permission from her in front of a counselor so the counselor can write a letter to the courts and say hey, both parents agreed that I could take them on vacation. And I know it was killing Lillith inside, because she's not able to go anywhere or do anything or take any vacations with the kids.

We didn't tell the kids where we were going. The kids had no idea what was coming up. We drive from Allentown to Baltimore where we're going to catch our flight to Fort Lauderdale. We let them go to the beach. Everybody's hanging out. Then we get on the plane and go to Fort Lauderdale. We spend 3 days there. Tensions were high, so I do my best to make sure Sprout and Lady are good. So anyway, we spend some time in Fort Lauderdale, spent some time in Miami. And then on Monday morning, we get ready to leave. We get in the rental van and we're driving back when we pull into McDonald's. We take the Disney shirts out, tell all the kids to close their eyes. We got a surprise for them. We put all the Disney shirts on, and we yell, "Hey, our vacation is just getting started. We're going on the Disney cruise."

Me and Bianca kind of parted ways on the cruise. Bianca did her own thing with her family, and I did my own thing with my mom and two daughters.

My kids are happy on the cruise. I feel like I got Lady back in my life. I told the girls, the ship is gonna have this, and Mickey's gonna do this and this other character is going to do that. Watching all the videos on YouTube, I started crying when I saw that. I was just very emotional the whole time on the trip. That first night, me and Lady can't sleep. We're too excited. In my cabin it was my mom sharing a bed with Sprout. Lady's sleeping on the other bed. I slept on the couch. So I hear Lady moving around and I'm like, "Lady, are you awake?" She's like, "Yeah."

I say, "You can't sleep either, can you?" And she said no. I'm like, "You wanna run around the ship? You wanna go play tag?"

That moment right there, I want my daughter back. Me and that little girl snuck out of the cabin. We run around the ship. We race up and down the stairs, with just the cleaning crews out. None of the other passengers. Just me and my daughter running free together on the ship, making up for lost time. I haven't been this happy in a long time. I tell her I'm sorry for everything, and I give her a hug. She says she's sorry, too. I got my daughter back. After almost a year, damn near $10,000 of working overtime, and I finally got my daughter back. We hugged it out. We both said sorry. She cried. I know she missed me. She wouldn't have cried like that if she didn't. We're standing on the top deck looking at the water. All you could see was the moonlight shining on the water. It's something I'll never forget. Obviously, it's very hard for me to talk about. Just all the sleepless nights and all the sacrifices I made. It seemed worth it.

So, anyway, we get in the elevator to go back to our rooms, and there's a sea captain and standing behind him was Micky and another character coming from rehearsal. Micky says, "Hi!" Lady gives him a hug. I swear, that little girl did not stop smiling until we left Florida. For the rest of the week, I lived on that moment. Me and her got to share that.

And I wasn't never going to let go.

One of the stops on the Disney Cruise was Cozumel, Mexico. Just me, my mother and my daughters walk into the boardwalk of the tourist attraction. As soon as we walk on the boardwalk, dolphins flip out. Lady looked back at me with the biggest smile. And I said, "You like dolphins, huh?" And she was like, "Oh my God, I love them!" She didn't know that I had paid for the excursion to go swim with the dolphins. So, we walk around then find a place to eat for about an hour, then it's our time. I said, "Alright Lady, I got one more surprise for you."

I tell them to put their life jackets on and we step down into the water. And here come two fins swimming right towards us. Of course, they got scared and they were standing face to face with dolphins. Lady had her hand around my arm. She was hugging me. She was so happy. I told her, "Go ahead, you can touch them." And she did. That was probably the biggest thing that had happened in her life at this point. We got to share that.

When we finished the Disney trip, Lady's back in my life like she was never gone. She's even sleeping over. It took a while for her to feel comfortable to sleep over again, but she was playing with the boys like nothing ever happened. So that told me she was brainwashed. I never heard Lady say that they did that. At this point, Lady never said it. It was coming from Lillith. But the brainwashing continued.

Me and Bianca made a lifetime of memories, and that year we traveled a lot. We went to Ocean City, MD. We went to Virginia Beach.

We planned a vacation to go the Myrtle Beach, Bianca and her four boys and her mother and father. I wanted to take Lady with us because I had a plan. This is in September. I wanted to take Sprout on a weekend vacation. And of course, her mother told me no. Lillith, as I mentioned before, never wanted me to do anything like that because she can't. But I had big plans for this trip. I planned to get engaged, and I wanted my daughter there for that. So, she took that away from me. She took that away from Sprout. I left from Allentown Airport and arrived in Nashville. Got out of the airport, jumped into my mom's car—she drove almost three hours to get to the airport—and we drove straight from the Nashville Airport to Myrtle Beach. I told my mom the plan was that I was going to ask Bianca to marry me. So, we stopped at a mall about an hour away from our destination, our timeshare. My mom helped me pick out a beautiful ring. I wanted my mom to be a part of all of it. I tell my mom I want to take out the whole family to a nice Italian restaurant, and "That song by Bruno Mars? I'm going to play it and then I'm going to ask her to marry me." So anyway, that was the plan. I had a big Bluetooth speaker and typed in my GPS the address of the resort and put in "Italian restaurants near me."

It wasn't even 2 minutes around the corner. I told Bianca, you guys make sure you're ready. Cause I'm an hour away and I'm hungry. We'll go there, unload, and then we can all take off and go find an Italian restaurant. So, everybody be ready. When we get there, we're going as planned, but before I got to the resort, I stopped at the Italian restaurant and I spoke with the owners and I said, "Hey, listen, I plan on getting engaged tonight here at your restaurant. This is what I wanna do, and I want to communicate with one of your servers. I have a Bluetooth speaker, and I want one of the servers to be holding it with a towel covering the speaker. What I'm gonna do is I'm gonna say I forgot my wallet. I'm gonna go outside to my car, cause we came in two separate cars."

When the time came, I went outside and got the speaker, the cook let me in the back of the restaurant, we were looking at the cameras. The owner was going to lead all the servers out and leave me standing in the kitchen.

The owner turns to me, "Ready?" and she goes out to the restaurant and says, "Ladies and gentlemen. I would like for everybody to join us. We have a very special moment happening here tonight. We are privileged to be a part of this." And as soon as the owner, moved her hand a certain way to give me the cue, I press play on the phone and the Bruno Mars song, "I Wanna Marry You," started playing. I chose that song because for many nights Bianca would watch videos on YouTube while I was going to sleep. Or I would pretend to be asleep, and I'd hear her listening to them. I would hear her crying and sniffling, being emotional. I wanted to give her that moment. That's just how much in love I was with this woman. Anyway, I played the song. And it plays through the Bluetooth speaker and everybody's clapping to the beat as I walk out. Very slow walk. I'm nervous. I'm shaking. After about 5 seconds, I seen Bianca's face. She knew what was going on, like I think she knew that because obviously I wasn't there at the table. She has her hand on her face. My mom was crying. Her momma's crying. Her son is crying. She's crying. And like I said, I was nervous as hell. I walk up to her. I give her a kiss on the cheek, get down on one knee, and I put the ring on her finger. And of course, she didn't even let me finish. She says yes, and I stand up and we hug each other, and she says, laughing, "What about our vacation?"

When we woke up the next morning together, it just felt different. I knew that this was my life. And I was willing to take on the challenge of her four boys, fighting my custody battle. All the outside noise was about to erupt. I think we both knew that. We wanted to show all over social media that we got engaged, she wanted to show her friends, her family, of course. But the demons were still out there. They were still attacking.

I'm getting sent screenshots of posts and pictures of the

other side those demons, including Lillith and Luke and Aunt Fiona. Constantly just making fun of us. Making comments. Making indirects. And of course, when you call them out on it, they deny it and say, oh, that's not about you. So, of course it is.

Bianca and I started fighting. The stress of all these attacks was too much. But still, we loved each other. There was no talk at this point of giving up.

HOW TO RUIN A GOOD THING

2015 - 2016

In 2016 I'm still at that Bar with No Name. I'm still at Coca-Cola, working second shift. I was no longer a temp employee, and I went from making $13 an hour to $21 an hour. I put in for 3rd shift because I wasn't gonna get first shift. I put in for 3rd shift because I wanted to watch every Cubs game. I wasn't gonna miss that game. I knew that I would be home during the day by myself. I knew that I would be able to watch the Cubs play and all I know is, I would get home at seven in the morning, help get the kids ready and off to their bus stop, come home and then I could sleep all day, right? That didn't go as planned.

Still, I was blowing up as a DJ non-stop. The clubs were packed. I had a large following, but my relationship with Bianca started to spiral downward. I made sure she was included in everything that I did as a DJ. I always wanted her there with me. I never hesitated to post pictures on social media of us at the club and she always had access to my phone. I never locked it, never put a code or anything because there was nothing she didn't know. I would fall asleep early, and she'd still be up, using my phone. Her phone was kind of trash. Whenever somebody messaged me, she always let me know. I never hid anything from her.

But then in 2016, all that started to go downhill. The attacks on us on social media never stopped. Our fights were getting horrible. Every time me and Bianca would fight, we'd go two or three days without talking. I would cry and sit in a corner and tell her I'm sorry, even if it wasn't my fault. But trying to deal with the kids, the four boys, I was basically in over my head. I started getting loud with them and intimidating and a little more physical with them than I should have, grabbing their shirts. I just started to lose it at this point. Bianca and I, we were in the same bed, but there were nights I was wanting her to sleep next to me or wrap our feet together or just let me know that she's there, But she usually just stayed on the phone and had her back towards me. Then I started finding out that she was in all these different chat groups, and she felt the need to let me know, hey, I posted a picture of us in my chat group and all these girls were complimenting you. Those were signs right there. Why do you feel the need to show me this stuff? I thought then I should get my own place and move, because driving from Allentown, Bethlehem, to the border of Breiningsville was a long drive after long days at work. And I had to do that every other weekend. At this point, I still wasn't seeing Lady, so it was just Sprout. She'd come over and all the kids would play and go crazy. There was a couple of nights where I would leave work on a Friday, and if I didn't have Sprout that weekend, I would go straight to the bar at Copperhead Grill, oh, around the corner from where we lived, and I would just sit there. If the Cubs weren't playing a late game when I got out of work at 10:30, then I'd sit there and just watch anything. I'd go in there just to have some kind of mental peace to myself sitting at the bar. Never had, never, never had a drink of alcohol or anything. It was always mozzarella sticks and soda. That was my stress reliever. I stress ate a lot. I didn't have the money funds to keep going to the gym to maintain my mental health so I was getting out of shape, too.

Things were crazy everywhere in my life. In April of 2016, I texted happy birthday to Lady and she came at me. I texted Sprout. Everyone was yelling and screaming at me. I got into an argument with my mom over the phone.

And of course it spilled into my relationship with Bianca. She gets home from work and hears all the yelling and screaming and I can see that she was just done with it. She was tired of hearing it.

I tell her, "My own fiancé, my own girl that I asked to be my wife can't even be there for me in a moment that I need her"

She left the room and went downstairs. My heart is pounding out of my chest now. All that trauma, everything that I've endured is building up, building up, building up. I don't know if it was a minor stroke or I was about to have a heart attack, but I couldn't breathe. I was crying. And I was trying desperately to scream for help. And I rolled off the bed and fell face first. And I blacked out. When I woke up, I had mucus, saliva, everything coming out of my face. And as I tried to regain my composure, I pushed up. I had a gray tank top on with red basketball shorts and brown flip flops. That was the moment that the old soft me had died. And I was born again as something much different, much darker. That moment that I woke up, and I recovered, and I came to and I regained consciousness. The demon had finally come out of me. The monster had been born. The monster had arrived. It said, "I'm taking over now because you're a pussy. You're soft." So, I carried that monster with me waiting to unleash. I went downstairs and I said, "I'm going to the courthouse and I'm fighting everybody and I'm going to tell them fuck you for what you did to me because I lost my daughter."

I went outside in brown flip flops. Red basketball shorts and a gray tank top. I walk out of the house and slam the door. And the next thing I know, Bianca runs outside, yelling "stop!" and she tackles me. Football tackles me from behind like I was a doll and like she was a guy. I'm on the ground and she's got all her weight on top of me, holding me down. And I'm crying and I'm screaming, and the neighbors are watching and I'm pushing with all my force to get away from her. We get in the car. She's driving. I'm shaking. I'm crying. I got veins coming out of places I didn't even know there were veins all over my face. I'm breathing heavy. Another traumatizing experience. Eventually I was able to come down. I sat at the table. She made a really good dinner. I remember the kids were acting up, jumping on the table, like we couldn't have peace at all. And she saw me starting to shake.

She sent all the kids to bed early and she came back, sat down and she grabbed my head and she's like, "I love you, don't you love me?"

When I looked at her, all I could say was, "OK." I threw my plate in the sink and went upstairs and laid back down because I wanted the day to be over.

That's the day that the demon inside of me was born. The monster that had its beginning with everybody fucking bullying me in high school, getting slapped around, getting spit in my face, to the 10 years of racial comments and all that shit that the blacks and the whites were doing to me for 10 years. And then *they* started bullying me. To all the shit that Lilith has put me through. And now I couldn't even have a normal home life. And maybe I realized I didn't know how to have a normal home life. Or maybe a normal home life was what I had and I was still chewing on the fantasy of what normal home life meant. Whatever. The monster was born that day and it came out roaring.

I said to Bianca, "I'm gonna walk out of here because I've never hit a female in my life and if I hit you right now, I'm gonna knock your fucking lights out and you're not gonna wake up for days." I slammed the door and looked around and I said "I am finally free from this fucking hell hole." That was the normal home life I was talking about. And I went out.

That's it. So that's November of 2016. So. As I'm trying to get my life back together and get my life adjusted, I'm still working third shift.

So, like I said, as 2016 went on, the fights were getting louder, and I started going into rages and breaking bedroom stuff. Frankly, the damage had already been done. All that dark shit that Brenda and Lilith planted on that radio show was growing, festering. There was no trying to page up or put a Band-Aid on everything that everybody done to us for the last two years. All the blasting on social media, fake Facebook pages, sending Bianca messages about how I was here, I was there and they see a car similar to mine and they would write to her, "Oh, your man just left with this girl, he's got a girl in his car" and meanwhile I'm lying in the bed right next to her while they're sending her these messages. It was continuous. It was nonstop. And I continue to further damage our relationship with my rages, and no matter how many times we tried to escape and have time just for ourselves there was no fixing it.

I ended up going to 3rd shift so I could watch the Cubs games. I just wanted to watch my baseball games because I knew Chicago was going to win the World Series. I predicted it. I knew it was going to happen. I had multiple conversations with multiple people and that's what I was most excited for and looking forward to. It was something that I was holding on to. Something was going to go right for the Cubs because it sure as hell wasn't going right for me.

Bianca took me to the Cubs Mets game in New York. When we were there, I realized that I needed sports to distract my mind. Like, I need to lock myself in my room as long as the Cubs are playing and the Bears are playing and the Bulls are playing. I don't have to worry about anything going on outside. I'm home. I'm in my room. I'm not out messing around or even trying to give anybody else attention. My attention was focused on the teams. I'm thinking we have a really good shot at doing something I've been waiting for my whole life.

In September of 2015, after we got engaged, the Cubs had lost in the playoffs. And I knew at that time that this time next year, the Cubs are gonna win the World Series! Like I was already manifesting, and I was already predicting it.

There were times, in the winter of 2015-2016 that I would come home and just sit outside and freeze. Because I knew that my team was going to win the World Series and I had to figure out my life because I knew that I was going to use that moment to change my life. I desperately needed peace to do what I needed to do to make me happy. All that was in the back of my mind, trying to be in a relationship. The sports was kind of a way to take my mind off of what was really going on in my life.

The reason I bring that up so much is I wanted to use that as a turning point in my life where something happened that I never thought would happen: the Cubs winning World Series. Is this a big deal? Yes. Sports fans, passionate sports fans, they understand what it meant for that to happen. So that's what I was looking forward to. I already knew in the back of my mind when 2016 started that I was gonna do whatever it takes to go to games, watch these games. And I did it all. Anyway, I mentioned that because it's going to play a big role in the change of events that takes place later in the year.

THINGS UNRAVEL

So, I'm still not seeing Lady, but I'm getting Sprout, and like I said, I need to leave this house because I can't take not seeing Lady anymore, it's getting ridiculous. And me living with Bianco was the reason Lady said she wasn't coming around. I was having multiple meltdowns at work, breakdowns of crying in the shower, I want Lady, I want Lady! And I was getting the opposite. I was getting horrible messages from Lady. Lillith was relentless in her effort to bash me on social media, beat me down and it just all built up along with the fights with me and Bianca. As one last attempt to rekindle our relationship. I mean, Bianca decided that for our birthdays we would do something special, because her birthday is July 19th and mine is July 20th. We were going to take that week and spend it in the Dominican Republic. Because she wanted me to see her country, where she came from. We booked the flight in the summer of 2016.

The first time I ever flew was when we took the family on the Disney Cruise, and that got my fear of flying out of my system. Now I would jump on a plane. On March 16th, I flew to Tennessee, surprised my mother for her birthday. It was a big surprise. I surprised my grandmother. And they were so happy to see me. The video that damn year went viral. I was flying to Chicago. I went to see my family again. I went to a few Cubs games with my cousin and that that was bringing me peace and I started feeling like, OK, now that I know that I can fly to Chicago and be there in two hours, it was kind of like mental rejuvenation for me. Cause mind you, I haven't seen my family from 2011 to 2016, so it was then 5-6 years that I didn't see my family, which was another thing that was killing me, killing me inside.

So anyway, me and Bianca went to the Dominican Republic, to Puerto Plata. We seemed to be determined to go through with our marriage and we decided that we were going to do our engagement pictures that week. She got in touch with the photographer, and we picked out our outfits, we took pictures on the beach. We went out for our birthdays that night and it was, I would say 99.9% adult resort that we were staying in so there were no kids. She thought it was okay for her to stare at guys, which I had some difficulty with. I was jealous because it was my first real relationship. But because we're on vacation, she convinced me that if a guy walks by and he's big and has muscles, she's gonna look. So, I was like, then I'm gonna look away. But it goes both ways. If I see a beautiful woman dressed in a bikini, I'm gonna look and I'm gonna admire, too. She was OK with that. July 19th we were at a bar. We had multiple drinks. I mean multiple, multiple drinks. Guys were walking around, and I was letting her enjoy her eye candy. But then, I remember, a girl walks right in front of me and I looked. I admired it. But I know that it was just gonna cause a problem. So I was like, forget it. Then she went off on me. We got into a huge fight, and she left the bar, so now I'm spending my birthday by myself. So, there were these two girls from New York, and I started talking to them.

At that point, when Bianca started arguing with me, I couldn't wait just to get back to the States, get back to Pennsylvania so I can pack up and move out. That was my immediate reaction. I still didn't know how to finesse situations. When things got tough, my response was to leave. So, after Bianca left, I met these two girls. We walked the beach together. They invited me to their room. Two girls, beautiful women. I had the chance to go back to their room. I couldn't ask for anything better, to have fun on my birthday: two beautiful women. I said, "Hey, give me a second. I'll be right there."

They walked up to their room, and I left. But I couldn't follow them. I want to do this the right way, not take out my anger by doing something stupid. I played it smart as intoxicated as I was. I ended up finding a little outside bed on the beach and passing out. I was there for about 2 hours until the security guard walked by and woke me up and said I wasn't allowed to be there because that part of the beach was closed.

I go back to the room and of course she's sleeping. I climbed in next to her.

When we wake up, we didn't speak. We have an excursion plan, and I was determined to go on it. But, my heart wasn't in it.

On this excursion, we hike two miles up the

mountains and then we jump off 11 different waterfalls until into water below. And we did all that and I was jumping as if I didn't care about life anymore. My last jump was a 34-foot waterfall. In the whole group of 18 people, only three people did it. I didn't hesitate. I was one of the three because I didn't care about the consequences. I went first. I was thinking, if this is my time, I'm ready to go.

When I get back to Bianca, I was in a slightly better mood. Physical activity does that to you. "Let's try to enjoy these last two days," I say, forcing a smile, even though inside I'm still pissed off.

Later, we take our engagement pictures, but there's this tension between me and her. The photographer makes us do these romantic poses and kisses and we went along with it. I felt like I was kissing her goodbye. Even though these are engagement pictures, I know we're not going to get married. My relationship is garbage, has completely fallen apart. I'm still dying over not seeing Lady. I'm still hurting because I know what I have to do when I get back.

Happy birthday to me.

FINALLY, A WIN!

When we get back to the states, I put in for first shift and I had enough seniority that I thought I would get it, and then I could get the apartment in the complex down the street from where my kids were. I passed those apartments for three years when picking up my kids, and I would always admire those apartments from the highway. I manifested and said I'm going to live there one day. By any means necessary.

So, when I got back from the Dominican Republic, I went in.

"Hey, listen," I said, "I'm in a big custody battle. I stopped by just to inquire. Like, how much is the rent. How much do you need in advance."

The apartment manager told me he had to do a credit check and would get back to me. I got a phone call about two days later and they say, "Hey, we've been able to approve you, but because your credit score is so low, you have to pay first month, last month, and security deposit up front."

"Okay," I said aloud, but I was thinking, "Holy Jesus, how do I afford that? What do I do?"

I did what I always do. I worked, I deejayed, and I

saved every penny in a separate account. Bianca and I had put our accounts together. Hence the reason I was always broke.

But now I was hiding my money. Any paychecks that I got from the club where I deejayed I would hide away. Private gigs? That money was hidden until I saved up almost $6,000. Bianca had a feeling that I was going to be moving out, but we aren't fighting anymore. I think it was a relief for both of us.

And I got approved. I could move in September 1.

I broke down crying, finally at peace. I called my mom and grandmother and made arrangements to come to Tennessee and move them out to Pennsylvania with me. When I got there, they hadn't packed anything. I rented a big moving truck, Penske yellow truck 26-footer, the biggest truck I've even driven. It took me about four hours to pack everything myself. I picked up furniture by myself, everything by myself. I ended up hitching my momma's SUV onto the back of the truck. I was on a mission. I was going to have a family. There was no stopping me. We drove two days halfway across the country, back to Pennsylvania.

My first stop was the new apartment. I get the key, and I walk behind the apartment, sit down on the curb and cry. This is it. This is what I need to get my daughters back in my life.

It took me a couple days, of course, to empty the Penske truck and get my mom and grandmother settled upstairs in my new apartment. But we're in.

I'm on 3rd shift and a couple of my coworkers come

together to take over my spot so I can go out to the trucker's locker room to watch the Cubs win the World Series. I break down, crying. It's my time. The Cubs won the World Series, doesn't that prove it? Everything's lining up.

My family's texting. I got about 100 text messages and calls, people saying, "I'm happy for you. I'm so happy. Like you deserve this. You deserve to be happy." They know how much I was going through, with me leaving Bianca, with me fighting for my kids, they knew that. I had a little bit of happiness and finally a little bit of hope that all the bad stuff was behind me. Everything I waited for, I manifested, I predicted….it's happening. Cubs win the World Series!

Now it's time to get my life together. I got my apartment. Everything's falling into place.

ONCE MORE INTO THE TRENCHES

I filed in August, and me and Lilith have to go to mediation. She knows how to play the system, taking her cheap shots. Again, she's saying that my family in Chicago, certain individuals in my family were saying that I needed help. "He needs mental help. He's crazy. He's unstable," she tells the mediator who nods slightly. Doesn't disagree.

But here's the thing: She's verbally abusing me in the mediation room and I'm the one who needs help? I was going crazy? Damn right I was going crazy. I lost the love of my life. I lost my future, because you guys ruined it.

She's making all these lies up again and, of course the mediator argues with me. Because now we're in 2016 and I really need to emphasize that Lillith is not getting in trouble for how she parents our kids. In 2013, they missed 18 days of school. In 2016 they missed 28 and 29 days of school. In 2015 they missed 26 days of school. Lillith isn't working. How are my kids missing almost 30 days of school every year? And there's no repercussions.

Since I had Sprout and I was taking her to school on Monday mornings, how is it fair? They have the nerve to tell me that I'm contributing to those. She never missed a day. I always dropped her off at her mother's house in the morning, almost an hour before her bus came. So I drop her off to her mother's custody and her mother doesn't send her to school, and it's my fault? The court system blames me and said I'm contributing to those absences. So you're telling me that five times, part of the 30 days that my daughter Sprout missed, that I dropped her off at her mother's house, on those days she was either late or never went into school. They said I contributed to that. How the hell? I dropped her off more than an hour early to her mother's house. They found a way to blame me for that too.

We can't come to an agreement because I filed seeking joint physical custody. One week with me, one week with my mom or one week with her mom. All switches would be made at 5:00 PM every Sunday. This was a pre-filing because I figured if I filed now, by time the court hearing came, I would already have my apartment. It worked out just like that. I have an apartment down the street from my kids. I need to be with them more than a few hours every weekend. They also want to live one week with me, then one week with my mom. My mother will also be taking care of my kids from 10:00 PM at night, because I was still on 3rd shift till 6:30 in the morning. I would have had my kids in bed at eight o'clock. They would have been asleep by the time I drove around the corner, because my job was only 5 minutes the other way. Mom's house was 5 minutes the other way from where I live. I lived in the middle of where my kids live and my job. Five minutes both ways. So anyway, what I filed was that my mother would be the one to take care of my kids, which all she had to do was be there when they were sleeping. I would be home at 6:30 AM to make them breakfast. Brush their hair. Get them dressed, drive them to school. I didn't need to put them on a school bus because I wanted to drop my kids off at school. That's what I was looking forward to. I have also changed my work schedule. I want to switch custody every Sunday at 5:00 PM. So, I filed it. Court hearing in front of the Honorable Edward Liebman, October 10, 2016.

My lawyer at this point was Michael David, a young man who just graduated from Yale Law School looking for his first big case. Wanted to get his hands dirty. He fought tooth and nail. Has all my respect till this day. The man was dripping sweat from his armpits, the knot of his tie was down into the middle of his chest. His smooth slick gelled hair was combed over to the side of his head. He sweated so much because of the demonic presence that was in that courtroom in front of Judge Liebman.

They gave me the chance to speak to the Judge. I explained that my intention was never to take the kids away. All I've ever wanted was 50/50. I lived down the street from them. I take care of my mother. She is disabled, but she is more than willing and more than able to stay with my kids and watch them while they sleep. She can cook for them. She wants to wake up and make breakfast for them, help them with their homework.

We left the courtroom. I was smiling.

They denied me.

Why should that be taken away from me? I work while they're asleep. While they're in school, I sleep. So why am I not being granted this? Their mother is saying they don't have their own room. OK, so I can't have my daughters. I told the judge I'm willing to sacrifice. My bedroom in my large two-bedroom apartment. That has a bedroom that's just half the size of the entire apartment itself. Then you got my mother's room. On the other side of the apartment, there's two bathrooms, so everybody has their own privacy. There's multiple closets, like there's room for all their clothes. I gave them a whole large closet for just their clothes. And I still got denied. Because, Lilith is arguing, pleading, that they don't have their own room. They need to sleep alone. They need to sleep together. Meanwhile, in the trailer, I'm telling the judge that Luke, Lilith, Lady, Sprout, Luke and Lilith's daughter Anastasia and their stepbrother, Alfredo, Luke's son, are all living there. So, my daughters don't have their own room in the trailer park. My apartment is three times bigger than the trailer park. So why? Why am I not allowed to have my kids?

Because they're missing 30 days of school. I'm just lazy, I sleep all day. They know this because they asked her. You just asked her. Dude, why don't you ask her why my kids are missing 30 days of school? Five of them were excused absences. The other 20 something were unexcused. So, when asked on this date why did your child miss these days, I couldn't answer. I dropped them off at their mother's place an hour before the bus. But somehow it's my fault.

I went to the school, and I got a print out and a report. My kids were not doing good in school, because they were missing so much time. The school, Fogelsville Elementary was frustrated. They told me, "We are tired of the excuses. We don't know what else we can do. We've reached out to the state. And for some reason, she's still getting away with it. I wish we could help you more, but legally we are not allowed to step over certain boundaries."

I am a desperate father trying to see my kids. My kids are missing 30 days of school, and you can't step over boundaries to help me and help my kids. But I'm not gonna make a big deal because she's an enemy to you too. We have a mutual enemy. So I have to work with the school now.

Anyway, I took that in front of the judge. I said, "The school is getting frustrated with having to deal with her. They don't want to deal with her anymore." But again. Because mom doesn't have a job, and I work and I'm taking care of my disabled mother, I can't have my kids. But it's OK for them to have a large pit bull and five other people in a tiny trailer. That's OK. I don't even think they let my lawyer talk because of the way I was talking in court, the way I presented myself, my wording, my professionalism. I was my own lawyer. I'm on my third lawyer, by the way. Why is he not helping me? Anyway, we left. They didn't give me my rights.

This is October of 2016. My lawyer looks at me and he says, "This was beyond my jurisdiction. That bitch is psychotic. She's crazy. Good luck the rest of the way. I'm going to get a drink." Those were his final words to me as we walked out of there.

THE BREAKUP WITH BIANCA

Although I had my apartment, in the fall of 2016 I was occasionally staying with Bianca if she needed me for something. I was driving all over creation going to work, going to pick up Sprout, so it was a good place for me to take a break sometimes too.

This one time, she wanted me to be home with her kids so after work I drove there, and I went upstairs to lay down. And at least get an hour of sleep, because I had just drove all the way from Breinigsville where I had dropped Sprout off. It was my custody day.

Bianca was working double shifts. She had already taken on two jobs, so she was hardly ever home. Even when I was there, she was working 16 hours a day and so on that Sunday she left her kids home alone. Because her mom had moved out with her sister and they had got their own little apartment down the street.

So anyway. Bianca's sons were picked up by their father and dropped off, and all four boys were home alone by themselves. She should have made arrangements, but she didn't And I'm laying down, trying to get a little sleep. When she comes in the house, bangs on bedroom door then kicks it open.

Apparently her kids had clogged up the toilet and it was all over the bathroom floor because they didn't think of the consequences of this toilet overflowing. Obviously I was unaware of it, so she came at me about it.

Now, mind you, I told you about the demon. The demon came out of me and I chased Bianca down the stairs with my fist cocked back and she locked herself in the bathroom. I was going to punch a hole through the door, grab her by her hair when I caught myself. I stop. And I put my face on the door, and I just kind of pushed the door lightly. And I said, "This is my green light to get the fuck out of here." So again, I left. I threw all my work clothes into a suitcase.

I was in a rage when I got back to the apartment, and my mom was trying to get me to calm down because it was stressing my grandmother out.

2016 ENDS WITH A BANG

Bianca was ready to end it one week and then she would call me crying and say I don't want to do this. Can we please, can we please make this work? Come November, Cubs win the World Series. Bianca calls me and she's crying, and she says I can't believe we're not watching this game together.

I was back and forth still, seeing her here and there. I did miss her. We needed our time away, which we should have done. But again. I didn't know how relationships worked. This was my first real relationship, but since it wasn't working, I thought my only solution was to leave. I'd DJ at the *Bar with No Name*. One of my female friends goes with me and we're partying and I'm deejaying. She's out there with all her friends. People see us leave together, and I took her to her car. We didn't do anything. At this point, I don't even care about life.

I was drinking and driving nonstop. I didn't care. I will get home. And then there was another girl who was messaging me in Facebook Messenger and I never met her in person. But me and her were talking and we were complimenting each other. Oh, you look nice. I saw your pictures. You look nice. And I was like, oh, I like that sweater, you look gorgeous in that sweater. Bianca hacks into my Messenger, she sees these messages. The night after I DJ at the club. I'm super hungover. I'm sick. I got a massive headache and I'm trying to sleep, and Bianca's calling. She called like 20 times and she's texting me. I call her and she says, I need you to come over. I need to go to the hospital. She's like, something is wrong with me. I need your help. Please come take me to the hospital. This is November 2016. When I get to Bianca's house, she's sitting in the corner. She's drinking from a bottle that we bought in Dominican Republic. I saw the anger, the hurt, the hatred. I saw the frustration in her face. We went at it. I took her keys out of my pocket, I turned around and I slammed them up against her wall, leaving a little bit of damage in her wall. She's like, I saw you were talking to these girls and this and this and that, and I know you were out at the club with a girl and you left with her, trying to accuse me, blah blah, it's fine, whatever.

The whole time between September and that day, November 16, I would get off work from the 3rd shift, wait an hour for her to leave the house to go to work, and I would go in there and I started moving out my stuff. Little by little.

That night she said to leave her keys there. She doesn't want to see me ever again. She's going completely berserk. She bleached all my clothes. She had them in the bathtub, bleach all over them. I couldn't get the rest of my DJ equipment. I couldn't get my basketball cards. All my Chicago Bulls cards that I had been saving since I was, Jesus Christ, I don't know, five years old. That would probably be worth up to anywhere between 100 to $300,000 right now. She didn't let me get anything. I lost my surround sound. Half of my bedroom set was destroyed, but I didn't care about that. I destroyed the other half. As I headed out, I told her, "I'm finally free from this fucking miserable house. I'm tired of sitting in a corner. This house was never mine. I was just an extra income and a babysitter to you."

When I got back to my apartment, I climbed the stairs and sat there before I opened the door. I embraced the peace and quiet. It was a Sunday night and I had just dropped Lady off. I would try to sleep for an hour on my mother's recliner, so she and my grandmother could sleep. My mom said as I was sleeping I would start shaking in my sleep and I had veins bulging out of my face.

I'm in a constant rage. I'm losing it at work. I'm talking to myself. One night at work some guy texted me telling me that if he ever sees me, he's going to kick my….. Original tough guy talk. Bianca's oldest son Harry, he had sent me a message telling me how horrible a person I was. Yadda, yadda yadda. I don't even think, I replied to him. And if I did, I'm not gonna argue with a 13-year-old kid. That's the way he felt. Then I started getting text messages from some number and some guy I don't even know who he was. Richard? He said he was Bianca's best friend. I've never heard of them. I was engaged to a woman, slept next to her for three years and I never heard of a guy best friend that she had? Don't threaten me. We went back and forth with bunch of gibberish, and I ended up blocking Bianca's number, blocking everything, blocking emails. No more contact whatsoever between me and Bianca.

I'm starting to lose it at work, arguing with people, and falling asleep on the job. I sleep in my car at lunch and both of my breaks. Drinking Red Bulls and energy drinks and doing whatever I could to stay awake at this point.

My third shift time is over. After the Cubs won the World Series, I want to go back to first shift. I put in for first shift.

Anyway, in the middle of December 2016, Lilith tells me that she's getting a job at Giant. OK. Good for you. She's working part-time 4 hours. Her second day at work. My mom and grandmother were gone. I get a knock on my door. Who the hell is it? It's Lilith. Yeah, so now she's coming over. And I'm sure I had a feeling I'm like, what are you gonna do about work? She said she needed to stop by and talk to me before she went to work. She said that her car died because Luke switched the battery cable and didn't want her to leave the house, but she managed to drive down the street, come to my house. So I knew what was about to happen. We were in my apartment alone. I hit record on the tablet, hiding behind the teddy bear and boom. Since Luke wanted to play this little game, here we go. She wasn't going to work. She was coming to my house. She still wanted me. She still missed me. And she was telling me how she wanted to divorce him. She was talking to a divorce lawyer, and she didn't want to be there no more. I was just letting it happen. I didn't care. I didn't care. This was me getting the ultimate payback. Because one day, for all the bullshit that he's done to me, him bashing me, him being the father of my kids and assisting with keeping my daughters from me, my daughter is following his rules, calling him daddy. Now it's payback time. Lilith's coming to see me because she misses me.

But when you confront Lilith about that, she says, I was

confused. Like please. Anyway, she was coming to see me. I was recording it. Whatever went down, I was recording it.

And I mean I recorded EVERYTHING. I wished she'd leave. That she'd be out of my house. I was so disgusted. I remember taking a hot shower. Scalding hot shower. I remember the burning sensation in my throat from wanting to throw up. But it was my way of payback because obviously the courts were doing shit for me. They weren't letting me see my kids. Because of that, not only am I getting my payback, I know that I'll get to see my kids now.

So guess who wants to start coming over and visiting her grandmother and great-grandmother? Suddenly Lady's back in my life. That's the sacrifice I had to make. Lady comes to my house. All Lilith wants is to... In return I get to see my daughter. How fucked up is this world? Because the courts don't see that. The courts are built for the women, so I had to play the street game now. And allow Lilith into my apartment.

Yes, she got a job for 4 hours every other day, three days a week. But she never went to that job, so they fired her. She's still found the way to sneak out to come see me. It's all on video.

But at least I was getting to see Lady again. At least I got my relationship back with Lady. So now we go back to counseling. Now that everything's fine, one or two counseling sessions because it's demanded by the court order.

So that was my 2016. I hope you enjoyed it just as much as I have.

2017 THINGS ARE LOOKING UP

So as we come into another new year, I'm still taking care of my mom and my grandmother and you-know-who is still sneaking over to my house. Still sending me nasty pictures and text messages blah blah blah. From September of 16 all the way up until January of 17, I was sharing a one bedroom with my mom and grandmother and we're on a wait list to move and we ended up getting a two-bedroom very large apartment. Plenty of room for my mom and grandmother in one room. And then I had the other, separate, bedroom all to myself. We had a good thing going there and so Lady is coming over and now I'm seeing Lady all of a sudden, and Sprouts coming and they even started bringing Anastasia, Lilith's and Luke's daughter to my house. I was taking them all out to eat, treated her as if she was my own. I'm getting to see my daughters plus their daughter. Obviously what's going on. Luke worked all day. I worked second shift. I'm really hating myself right now for allowing the intimate part between me and Lilith. But it's a trade-off. To see Lady, I had to be with her mother.

I was very, very disgusted with myself. I hated myself. I couldn't even look at myself in the mirror. There wasn't enough soap and hot water to wash off. That's how disgusted I felt.

At the same time, my DJ name was still blowing up. I have

a lot of women who were after me. A lot of women trying to hook up with me . I don't know how to explain it, but I was disgusted with my life that it was so dark.

But nobody was around, so yeah, I'm just going with the flow. January is a continuation of 2016 obviously. Me and Lady are getting closer again and I can tell she missed me because she started opening up to me about things that any normal teenager would. She even opened up to me about her sexuality. She had a crush on a girl and didn't know if that meant she was lesbian. Live and let live, I say, plus I have lots of friends in the LGBTQ community, so I don't bash it. But I told her she was still young. She didn't have to make a life-time decision at 15. Or ever for that matter. It really made me happy that Lady felt she could confide in me about that.

But, I'm still hurting that I lost Bianca. I'm still angry about the way it ended. And I wanted retaliation. I was literally stuck in my own head. Making up conversations of what I would say to Bianca if I got the chance to face her again. I was just playing the role with Lilith.

In the meantime, Lilith tells me that she's filing for divorce and that she was speaking to a divorce lawyer. She was talking really bad about Luke. She accused him of messing with a girl while she was there and that he exposed himself to a girl at the trailer one night as well as Lady. But Lilith is the world's greatest liar, so I didn't really believe it. Lilith wasn't happy and so she was making up stuff. I was like, I felt bad for Luke because, even though he supported my daughter being kept away from me and he made threats and all that other stuff, he deserved better. But honestly, I didn't care. I didn't care about what I did with Lilith for those few months. That was payback for keeping my daughters away from me.

Me and Lilith continue our affair. She was going to the clubs where I was deejaying and taking pictures with me and showing off and saying this is my baby daddy, because the name was blowing up and she wanted a part of it. She and my mom got really close, and my mom fell for her BS. I knew in the back of my mind, while I had everybody telling me don't fall for it, don't fall into her trap. I knew exactly what I was doing. I thought.

Fast forward to April of 2017. Lilith comes over with Lady, Sprout, Anastasia, and Lady's best friend, Mariah. We're hanging out when Lilith gets a call. She jumps from the couch and runs outside. She comes back as if she's seen a ghost. Obviously Luke knew she wasn't home. He knew she was hanging out at my house. He started drinking again and got caught drunk driving for the fifth time. Later, during his eight-hour court hearing, when he was on the witness stand, he was confronted about it, and he said, "I was not there for her like the man I was supposed to be." I kept my mouth shut. Because all this time he could have told her enough with the drama, keep the fuck out of my house or trailer.

But he didn't. Obviously he's not me.

Like I said, he gets picked up for drunk driving again and Lilith is frantic, and she leaves. So, I'm stuck with the kids. I thought it was funny because he had a record and that gave me confidence that I was going to have my kids back. It was something I could use in court, right? Because, in my mind, the courts would obviously say, hey, this is a messed-up situation that the kids are in and if this guy is constantly drinking and driving then the kids are in a dangerous situation. What if he's intoxicated, has the kids in the car, and he crashes and kills somebody? That's what a normal human being would assume that the courts would think.

And now is my golden chance now to get custody of my kids. Right? No. So she's continuing to collect child support while still coming over to my house. She was still asking me for money. But everybody knows that he was sending her money, and his job was giving her money. Her family was giving her money. Because she played victim instead of just getting a job and supporting her kids. She couldn't do anything for herself. She never wanted to get a job. She never wanted to work. But she's on social media saying that she's the world's greatest mother since time began.

But anyway, I was giving her money on top of child support. And it got to a point where the trailer had rats and mice and roaches. It was very nasty. I kept those messages, and I made screenshots of them because I knew one day we'd have to go back to court, and I needed the evidence of her lifestyle. I tell her, take me off child support, and I'll help you, and I'll give you money so that you can get the trailer cleaned up and get mouse traps as well as all the beers that you're asking me for.

My mom was going over there helping with the kids because she wants to see her grandkids. And my mom developed a relationship with Anastasia, who was calling her grandma. I didn't understand this relationship at all. Why are you getting attached? It was hard for me to deal with that. My mom was going over there, but my mom was getting information as well.

Do you remember back in 2014 the radio show that they all did against me? Wait till you hear this. Brenda had stiffed Gloria, my great good friend and photographer, my sister so to speak, for a couple of gigs and Gloria started to get the feeling that something wasn't right, so she hired a private investigator to look into Brenda. They found out that Brenda, the wedding coordinator and the one who did the radio show about me saying I like little kids, has a not so perfect resume. The private investigator had a pretty detailed report. Brenda has never disclosed that she was born in the Dominican Republic. That's because Brenda wasn't. A man named Bernardo Macias Bisla was. That means, she had the surgery, and she had implants and apparently a major reinvention. What about all those fundraisers about having cancer and all the money she collected and all those benefits she was throwing, making herself seem like she was some goddess of the community? She was pocketing all that money. She needed it to continue the surgeries and have facial hair removal.

I couldn't believe it. I knew something was up way back in 2014. It explained why her boyfriend was the way he was. She was born a man and those two kids that she claimed were hers were not hers. Nobody knows who they belong to. Apparently she left the Dominican Republic with them.

She claims she adopted them. Till this day, nobody really knows. So Gloria went on and on about it and exposed Brenda publicly. I still have the messages. Lilith, who was still friends with these people was showing me pictures of the surgery.

It turns out that Brenda was accused in the Bronx with molesting a three-year-old boy. Which is why she came to the Lehigh Valley. People were looking for her.

Everything that Brenda accused me of is exactly what she was guilty of. Brenda and her husband up and left town after she got exposed. How's that for some soap opera?

The image of Brenda with my kid at the courthouse in 2015 came roaring back. She offered to take four-year-old Lady to the bathroom. Lady was getting loud. It was a long boring day. At the time, I didn't like the way she was holding my daughter, hands up between her legs. Taking her picture. That's something I have to live with. All those pictures that Brenda took.

And the courts allowed my daughter to stay with her mother who was great friends with Brenda. Who allowed this to happen?

Is it wrong to say that I would love to run into Brenda again someday and beat the crap out of her? This is one of the top issues that caused my rage. I only hope one day my kids realize how ignorant and foolish their mother was to allow this to happen. That she allowed our daughter to be alone with a psychotic animal.

I even made a post about it on FB. Which is totally unlike me. I like to keep my social media upbeat and professional.

Some fun stuff about my kids and sports. But I made a post. That was my retaliation against them doing that radio show about me. Everyone who was on that radio show were brainwashed and got played for a fool by a child molesting transexual. So I hope they're all happy and I hope they can all live with their selves and make sure that they know that they fell victim and were brainwashed and fooled by somebody sycophantic and evil, a child molesting pervet named Brenda Bernardo Macias, DSLA. Those are the kind of people that they all like to roll with. That's fine. There's not enough apologies in the world. They couldn't even pay me enough money to ever forgive any of those people. They are enemies for life.

That was that and one of the few things I had to smile about. I'm still seeing my kids and Lilith is still texting me, very inappropriately, while I'm at work. If you go through the messages, you'll see I was not engaging in it as much because Luke was getting out in January of 2018.

But as the year was going by, I started developing nocturnal attacks. I never went to the doctors to get a diagnosis, but talking to people in the medical profession I got a good idea what was happening. There were anxiety attacks because of the trauma that I was suffering. Only a few people have seen me like this. One friend was giving me a ride home from a DJ gig at the Bar with No Name. I was intoxicated from drinking. She gave me a ride so I didn't have to drive, but as soon as we pulled up to my place, I burst out crying. My body tightens up for about 5 seconds and then it releases me slow. And this would go on for about four to six minutes. Then I would catch my breath curl up into a ball as tight as possible. I was clenching my teeth so hard, I'm lucky they didn't break. I would be locked into a fetal position for several minutes until the tension would subside.

It happened at night after I had a few drinks. Anywhere between 11:00 PM and 3:00 AM. I was getting these attacks nonstop. Once a friend brought me home and asked to use the bathroom. When she came into my bedroom to say goodbye, she found me on the floor having an attack.

Everything was too much. And I had no real emotional support. I found myself missing Bianca because, as much as I knew we were over, she was the first real emotional support I ever had in my life. Imagine that, in my entire life I only had one person who gave me emotional support.

How's that for a reality check?

AND LOOKING DOWN AGAIN....2017 ENDS

My emotional state was getting worse. I was going crazy. I get caught several times talking to myself at work, at home. The kids see it, and I think I'm scaring them. In my car I'm yelling and screaming, replaying traumatic scenes in my head. I finally go to a doctor, and he diagnosed me with severe anxiety, severe depression. He prescribed pills, but they just messed me up. Made me a zombie.

The year was flying by. The good news was that Lilith and Lady were always coming over. I wanted to spend New Years with them because I know it would be the last one. But Lady wants to spend New Years Eve with her friends.

"Why are you leaving? Why can't you spend one New Year's with me?" I exploded.

Lilith doesn't take my side. In fact, she says nothing.

The next day, January 1st, Luke was getting released from prison. Clearly, Lilith wanted to be there for him. I drag Lilith outside so the kids don't hear us

"This is how you're gonna do and why you have to act like this. And you're gonna take Lady away?" I'm like a madman.

Lilith opens the door so that Lady can hear the conversation. She wanted to make me look like I'm the bad guy in front of Lady.

I go back inside. That was the last time I seen Lady cause Luke got out the morning of January 1st, 2018.

2020 THE BEGINNING OF THE END

As we enter this new year of 2020, not knowing the world would be shut down, my year starts with the death of my grandmother. The hardest death I've ever had to deal with. I fly to Tennessee for the funeral in January of 2020 and can't get myself together for the hours I was in the funeral home. It hurt not only to know she was gone, but the anger and hurt I've held inside all these years stopped me from spending more time with her. I did, however, make sure she traveled everywhere with me and made some very memorable times the last two years of her life.

As I watched her being laid to her eternal resting place, I thought about all the conversations I had driving around with her. Like sitting at a gas station drinking hot chocolate, just crying, venting to her about everything that was happening with my daughters. I know the dementia didn't allow her to process anything I was saying, but at least she was able to say things that defended me. That's all I needed, just someone to listen. Now that is gone.

During my time of grieving, I got a text message saying "sorry for your loss" from Lilith. I don't even reply because I think, if you're so sorry, why wouldn't you allow the kids to come spend time with her just to make her final moments a bit more enjoyable? Anyway, those are just some of the millions of thoughts I had going through my head at that time. Then here comes the "I'm going to cancel child support" messages once again. Took for my grandmother to pass away to have that taken care of!? Why should I be surprised!?

I knew I had to get myself together and finish my fight. I made my grandmother that promise before the casket closed.

I finally get a job in May when I get back to Pennsylvania after being out of work since July of 2019. I took my first management role at a place that would run my health and mental state into the ground over the next three years.

I can't express how being locked up in a big house with Sprout for the past few months became some of the happiest times of my life. Turning the house into an obstacle course, making the stairs a giant slide, etc. All we did was dress up in costumes and play around like two little kids during that time!

So, I'm back to working five days a week, lose the house as my lease was officially over and decide it's time to fight for fifty-fifty of Sprout one last time. My job was in complete support of my battle and gave me the time off to do what needed to be done. I rented another big house knowing I could not afford it, from another slumlord, not knowing a "friend" lived right across the street whose kids went to school with my little one, but also did homeschooling since we were on lock down. Everything's going in my favor right?

I file for joint custody in June. I made sure that I followed the letter of law in the family court system guidelines pertaining to joint custody.

- I need to reside in school district. Check
- I need someone to watch Sprout and help her with her online schoolwork. Check (with a detailed letter from the "friend" that she is licensed to operate a daycare)
- I need to have the extra bedroom for sprout. Check. I had 4 bedrooms)

Our court date is now set for August 2020. We had to go to mediation once again which was pointless. We didn't come to an agreement. Then we had pre-trial in front of the judge, and we didn't come to an agreement there either. Both lawyers got involved, and we're in full blown trial.

Wait? Did I just beat the system!? Hell, yes I did! I was granted fifty-fifty of Sprout exchanging custody every Sunday! It only took seven years, 30 hearings, and six lawyers to do so! When I left the courthouse, I sat in my car for two hours crying. Finally victory! A week on, a week off with my Sprout.

But let's address the text messages I was getting 3 weeks prior to the hearing...

Texts were flying in weeks before the hearing about "let's do this as a team" etc. Same things I have been trying to do for 7 years. I paid no attention and didn't reply, knowing anything I responded to would have been turned around on me and used in a negative way for the trial. But two days after the hearing when I thought it was all clear, I replied, "now we can talk."

Of course, we had to meet in a public park. Lilith and Lady came walking towards me. I got up to greet them and say, "Okay, now we can talk."

I don't know why Lady was there, in what was an adult situation, but suddenly she was attacking me because I wanted to spend more time with Sprout than her. She was screaming, yelling, cursing. I kept my cool, but hearing this from my first child was the most hatred I have ever felt. I couldn't believe it. But it was obvious where it was coming from.

"You didn't want to be part of my life for even two hours a week like the court ordered," I told her.

I knew this wasn't the end of it. As Lady was being dragged away, I called my lawyer yelling and screaming, called the counselor, yelling and screaming.

I finally moved on with life trying to adjust to my new schedule as a father. In September 2020, I took a vacation and met a lovely woman. Nine months later I got a double dose of fatherhood. The universe blessed me with boy and girl twins. I get to have another shot at being a father without the hassle and drama this time! But wait, as soon as this news breaks and of course, I receive one more act of retaliation and back on child support I go! Thus beginning two years of struggling once again until the final nine-hour hearing in December of 2021 that I talk about in the Prologue.

WHAT HAPPENED NEXT

Life goes on. Lady, the apple of my eye, got her mind filled with paranoia and lies about me. And I realized there was nothing I could do about that. No matter how many judges or mediators said that she had to spend time with me, no one was going to force her into it. Not Lilith. Certainly not Luke. Not when they were the ones telling her what a psycho I was.

In 2018, when I tried to contact her, she came at me screaming saying I wouldn't pay for her braces. It was the first time I heard she even needed braces. I think the head game that Lilith and Luke were playing with me was that they wanted to be the providers for Lady and Sprout, even though they weren't trying very hard to give them a decent life.

I tried several more times to get half and half custody of both Lady and Sprout. I had lots of support, including judges who were personal friends of mine, vouch for my character. But it didn't matter. The courts in Pennsylvania are convinced that only women are good parents and most custody battles in my state end up with mothers, no matter how bad they are, getting most of the custody.

One of the last times I was in court, I was the third in the docket, so I got to hear the cases in front of me. One was a woman who was a drug addict—needle type drug addict—fighting for custody of her kid. I thought, wow, maybe now I'll get some justice. But the judge, unbelievably, awarded her joint custody. I knew then I didn't have a chance.

By this time, I have been in court or mediation 36 times. I spent more than 60 thousand dollars on court and lawyer fees. I spent countless money trying to get apartments suitable for my kids and mom. It occurred to me more than once that kids who are living with two parents, they don't need separate bedrooms for everyone. They don't need parents to be there 24 hours a day, especially if they have a job, or jobs. It seemed so grossly unfair that I was working 2 jobs to afford child support and a nice apartment and outings for the kids, but that the courts held that against me. One because I wasn't home all the time, even though my mother was, and two because they were prejudiced against DJs.

It was easy to think that the system was rigged. After one court hearing, I see my lawyer go to lunch with Lilith's lawyer and it shocked me to tell you the truth. I was so enraged at what I considered a betrayal, fraternizing with the enemy! But then, I realized that the family court system was an entity that thrived on people, dopes like me, coming back to court again and again. It was literally how they stayed in business and kept their jobs. That 60 thousand that I spent on lawyer fees and court fees, would've been better spent on a downpayment to a house. If you ask me what I would do over, that would be it. I would keep my money out of the court merry-go-round and buy myself and my kids a house.

The longer I stayed in the system, too, the more I realized

how some people like Lilith learned how to game the system to their advantage. Their advantage being collecting child support. When it looked like I had a good case going into my last 50/50 hearing—lots of contempt evidence against Lilith, my own housing and job situation had significantly improved—Lilith made sure to prep Lady saying that I put my hand on her inappropriately while we were watching television. That shit is in the record, and it made me sick. This was the little girl I longed for. The little girl who swam with me and the dolphins, that I had gone through fire for to get even a weekend visit. And she was turning on me in the most grotesque way.

We had to have joint counseling, of course, and of course she never came. I lost her. One of my biggest fears was that without a good father in her life, that she would get pregnant before she finished high school. Any aspiration for a better life for herself was gone. And that's exactly what she did. It seems like one thing the judge had predicted in this battle had come true. She and her baby, her baby daddy, Luke, Lilith, Sprout, Anastasia, and pit bull live in their mobile home. It makes me sick, but I gave up my rights to her. I gave up my rights to Sprout too.

My big dream, as I said before, was to have a bunch of little kids running to meet me when I came home from work. And that part of my dream has come true. I met Eliza at a DJ gig during Covid, and we started dating. She had our twins in May of 2021. A girl and boy, Xander and Jasmine. While Eliza and I aren't a couple anymore, we coparent like civilized people. I live a block away and see them all the time.

They can, and do, come to see me anytime they want. Needless to say, the Pennsylvania court system isn't involved.

Another big dream of mine was to reconnect with my own father. We had been estranged when he broke up with my mom. I have been going back to Chicago a lot and recently we met up. He is a legendary DJ in Chicago, and I am proud to say he came to one of my gigs and seems to think I'm pretty good too.

I think now that when people talk about family, it's the emotional support they're talking about. It doesn't matter if you have a mother and father in one house, if they connect with you about things that matter, you are being supported. Same with partners. There is attraction, and that's important, but if you don't have each others' back, you're not a family.

There is no happy ending. The only good thing to come out of this are my twins! My son, my daughter! One last chance to be a father without any kind of drama involved.

Now I'm stuck with life-long mental trauma where, most days, I can't seem to get out of my own head.

Wondering if I can ever love someone enough to have somewhat of a healthy relationship. It's understandable that most people wouldn't understand the difficulty of trying to "love" again after losing not one, but two, daughters that I would have given my life for without thinking twice about it.

Every day is a struggle to block out the evil voices and scenarios being created in my head. But hey, nobody cares! Just continue to put on a fake smile and pretend everything is okay! I am with you guys in this silent battle of pain we face every day. Good luck on all your battles gentlemen, protect your mental health by any means necessary.

WHAT'S NEXT—FROM THE EDITOR
Epilogue

Sly is working now to try to get the laws of Pennsylvania changed so that custody doesn't unfairly favor the mother. One law, a couple of years ago, languished in committee and never made it to a vote. But now, as we go to print, we have another champion in the Pennsylvania state legislature, Congressman Jamie Flick (R-Lycoming/Union). A new law with a provision he introduced to a new bill will reduce the burden on families and courts by reducing the factors considered during child custody issues from 19 to 12. Gov. Josh Shapiro recently signed the measure, which Flick said was improved with his amendment to require family courts to provide anyone named in a custody petition with a written copy of the new factors when decisions are made. Flick's amendment, which was unanimously approved by the House, requires the court to give everyone a copy of the new factors within 30 days of modifications being made. The amendment was made to House Bill 378.

"Everyone involved in these cases must understand what factors the courts are considering when making custody decisions," Flick said. "This allows them to present relevant information and arguments. When both parties understand the criteria used by our courts, it levels the playing field."

Flick, a fierce advocate of 50/50 shared custody, noted

that once his amendment was added, it took just a little longer than a month for the Senate to unanimously pass the bill and Shapiro to sign it.

"I am pleased the governor supports my amendment," Flick added. "This fuels the momentum we are building toward reforming child custody laws."

Flick's own bill, House Bill 1499, would ensure fairness in custody and protect the rights of children to have equal access to both loving and fit parents. House Bill 1499 now has more than two dozen lawmakers who have signed on as cosponsors. The bill is also widely supported by constituents in his own district, throughout the Commonwealth, and across the United States, Flick has received hundreds of emails and thousands of comments on social media regarding his legislation. Including from this author.

"Republicans and Democrats are coming together on this issue because they recognize that custody decisions should put children first - not politics or outdated assumptions," Flick said.

House Bill 378, now Act 11 of 2025, should be in effect by the time you are reading this book.

There is some urgency to this legislation. Imagine you are a father who cannot have access to his children. He wants to be a part of his children's journey, seeing them grow, watching them laugh and responding to the abundance and possibility that is life itself. It is one of life's riches. A second chance to experience the joy of life itself. But more than that, he knows the damage that not having a present father does to children. Fatherless children are at a disadvantage as far as self-confidence and achievement, but there is nothing a father who is denied fair access to his children can do. The psychological damage is unimaginable. He cannot protect his children, even as his children are denied their father's protection. A society that claims the family is the basic unit of that society cannot go on tearing apart the unit that is its support.

Many fathers who do not have access to a loving relationship with their children become depressed, despondent and commit suicide. Lots can be said about the role of men in our current society, but it must be admitted that being denied the primary role of protective and guiding father is a huge blow to the identity of men. Period. Does that mean that women have to stay in relationships that no longer serve them? Of course not, no. But it does mean that everyone has to acknowledge that a strong male presence in a child's life serves the child, the family unit, and society. We all benefit when fathers are treated as equal coparents.

When Sly first started writing this book, he said his mission was to have hundreds of men, professionally assembled, marching arm in arm to the Lehigh County Courthouse, protesting the seemingly arbitrary way the family courts in Pennsylvania dispensed justice in family relationships. He finally decided a more powerful way would be to tell his story. Sly isn't a saint. God knows, no one is. But he is a man who loves his children, who provides for his children, who gives fatherhood a good and joyous name. If every third man, at least, had these qualities, society as a whole would benefit. We wouldn't have children spending their lives looking for the safe haven that should be their father, instead finding a more accessible safe haven in drugs, alcohol or other addictive behaviors.

Sly will be giving his author talks in the way he knows best....DJ and community events. I hope you will support him and hear his story. And help us advocate for a complete society. Blessings on you all.

ABOUT THE AUTHOR

Born and raised in Chicago, moved to Indianapolis Indiana raising his 2 daughters for 10 years, then followed the music to Allentown Pennsylvania where he's resided for the past 12 years due to its large population of diversity. It is here is where he went to war with the family court system for almost a decade.

www.ingramcontent.com/pod-product-compliance
Lightning Source LLC
Chambersburg PA
CBHW071222160426
43196CB00012B/2386